FOUR STEPS TO FUNDING

How To Avoid Rejection

And Get Your Proposal Funded On Your Next Try

By **Morgan Giddings**, PhD

FOUR STEPS TO FUNDING

How To Avoid Rejection And Get Your Proposal Funded On Your Next Try

By **Morgan Giddings**, PhD
http://fourstepstofunding.com/extra

Version 1.2, ©2011 All Rights Reserved

ISBN (978-0-615-50558-9)

WHO WROTE THIS

Morgan Giddings, PhD is a scientist and author who has written over 35 major grant proposals, and had a success rate well north of 50%, producing nearly $10 million in funding. Based on her experience with a series of grant rejections early in her science career, she vowed to learn the rules of success. After finding a mentor, learning some key insights, and applying them in combination with some hard work, she began having immediate success in applying for highly competitive science grants from the National Institutes of Health and National Science Foundation. She used the same principles to get funding to open a bike shop and a kayak manufacturing business.

After further developing the strategies for successful grant funding based on marketing principles, she began teaching those approaches to get more grants funded to other scientists.

The principles of a successfully funded grant proposals are universal, so this book is written for a wide audience to convey the core elements that make up any kind of successful grant proposal - for business, non-profit work, education, or research.

For any questions or support issues, you can reach us through the help desk at **http://support.marketingyourscience.com**

TABLE OF CONTENTS

INTRODUCTION

I opened the envelope with anticipation. Finally, I hoped, my grant would get funded. I'd tried three other times, each ending in rejection. I felt this time would be different.

I tore the envelope open, and looked at the single sheet inside.

"UN" - Unscored.

That is the worst possible outcome for a grant proposal to the National Institutes of Health (NIH).

It was near the end of 2003, and I was an assistant professor at the University of North Carolina at Chapel Hill. My fate rode on getting grants. In a few more years, I'd be coming up for tenure - a make or break point in my career. Without getting a grant or two funded, I had little chance of tenure.

But I'd just had four failures in a row. What to do?

I made an appointment to meet with a senior faculty member in my department. He did not comfort me. He told me that my approach to grant writing was all wrong.

It was a serious blow to my ego. I thought I was great. After all, I'd had multiple proposals funded before becoming a professor. But the game had changed. The bar was higher for these big research grants, the competition was fierce and funding was becoming ever more scarce.

After some soul-searching, I decided to ask the mentor for some deeper help. The first few sessions with him left me nearly in tears. My ego was shredded. I realized that I didn't have a clue how to write an effective proposal, but I was determined to learn.

Fast forward to five years later, and I'd just had my fourth big NIH R01 proposal funded in a fiercely competitive environment. This time, I scored in the top few percentage of all grants reviewed. The funding was all but assured. Right after that, I got another big award.

What changed?

It turns out that I had no strategic approach to grant writing, but I <u>was</u> good at one thing: putting myself in the mind of the reader. Unfortunately, I wasn't systematic about my process, so my proposals were hit-and-miss at best.

My mentor helped me systematize grant writing into an approach that conveyed my ideas clearly every time. It also changed my work approach altogether!

Rather than coming up with an idea, and saying "Hey, I think this is great, I'll try to write a proposal to get funding," I'd first ask myself: "Does anyone care about this particular idea? Who is the audience for this? How will it be useful to them?"

Later, I co-founded a bike shop with another family member. That landed me in the same desperate situation I was in after four grant rejections. We didn't know how to market the bikes. We got deeper and deeper in debt. It was very frustrating.

So I learned about marketing by purchasing a bunch of courses on the subject.

Then the lightbulb went on: marketing is not at all different from grant writing. They are one and the same activity. In a grant, you are marketing your future project or idea to a group of people, and trying to convince them to spend money on it.

Marketing has been studied extensively. I put the marketing principles to work to further systematize the art of grant writing, with great results. I started helping others get more grants and fewer rejections.

Once I learned the intersection of marketing and grant writing, I realized that four key elements stood out as essential in successful grants. I was failing to address one or more of these in each of my grant rejections. Once I changed my approach, the results improved dramatically.

This system really works. I've been using it all along, but until I understood it for the simple formula that it was, it was difficult to apply in a systematic way. The formula makes this easy. I believe you will find it as useful as I have for getting grants funded.

SECTION 1:

YOUR FRAME OF MIND DETERMINES YOUR GRANT FUNDING

CHAPTER 1
<u>Why</u> be a great grant writer

"Research is four things: brains with which to think, eyes with which to see, machines with which to measure and, fourth, money."

- Albert Szent-Györgyi

Writing successful grant proposals will be a major determiner of your success as a scientist, academic or nonprofit administrator. Grant writing is also an invaluable skill for new business owners, professionals and entrepreneurial types. In fact, being a great grant writer, and landing million dollar grants, is a valuable skill in any environment.

That's because in any human endeavor getting things accomplished requires one or more of three core elements:

- » **Time**

- » **Energy**

- » **Money**

I learned this principle from Mark Joyner, creator of Simpleology. I have yet to run across any other way that you can create success without at least one of these three elements.

Let's consider time. You can't make more time. Everyone has the same amount in a day. The only thing you can do is optimize your use of it, but you don't get more of it.

Next let's consider energy. You can become more energetic by optimizing the way that you live and through the foods you eat, but there are pretty strict limits on how much energy anyone can achieve.

Money, on the other hand, allows us to do extra work in an almost limitless fashion. The more money you get, the more you can enlist the aid of others in the work that you're trying to accomplish. This leverages your power in unrivaled ways.

So unless you're content to accept the limits of your own ability to move a particular project forward, you must have money.

In a company, money often comes from revenues. In a non-profit organization, research organization, or university, much of the money to fund expanded operations comes from grants.

CHAPTER 2
<u>What</u> is great grant writing?

There's a popular marketing quote that says: "The meaning of a communication is the **response that it gets**."

Given this quote, what is a rejected grant's meaning? Obviously, it wasn't what you intended, since you spent time writing it in hopes that it would get funded (and it didn't). That wasn't exactly the "meaning" that you had in mind.

It is pretty amazing that for just a few well-written pages, one might receive thousands or even millions of dollars (which are also paper or blips on a computer screen, but that's another topic).

The problem is that most novice grant writers assume that when a grant proposal is rejected, the problem lies externally. It is an "unfair system," we might tell ourselves, or "the reviewers are biased." We blame these issues, or some other circumstance that's beyond our control.

To put this in perspective, let's consider the advertising world. Let's say I work for an ad agency, and that I create an ad for a new automobile that is being introduced, the Denavio. Let's further say that my ad seems "brilliant" both to me and my colleagues. Yet when we put it out in front of customers and the public, the response is dismal, and we don't sell any cars.

What was the meaning of my communication? Whose fault is it that I didn't sell any cars?

Let's say that I'm fired by the car company because of my ineffective ad. They hire another agency, which comes up with an ad that actually sells cars.

Whose fault is it that my ad didn't work? Is it the "stupid consumer who just didn't get it?" Or was it my communication, which obviously didn't resonate with my audience?

My hope is that you'll be hard pressed to answer anything but "yes" to the notion that my communication simply didn't resonate with my audience, and that that's why the resulting sales were abysmal.

The situation is no different with a grant proposal.

The key is to learn from our mistakes, and to become better grant writers. Some of us (like me) come by this lesson the hard way.

When I started as a new faculty member at the University of North Carolina, I was told that I needed grants in order to get tenure. I took that message seriously, and started writing grant proposals right away.

The first one (to the National Science Foundation) was rejected. I revised it and resubmitted it. That one was rejected too, and with a score that was worse than the first one. Next I tried the National Institutes of Health (NIH), which rejected my first grant. The second one was rejected without review (the worst fate for a grant at the NIH).

"A great proposal is nothing more and nothing less than one that achieves the desired aim: to get the funding that supports the proposed project."

It took those four consecutive rejections for me to make a few crucial mental shifts. Forgetting the notion that I could just "figure it out" on my own because I'd been successful in the past was the first shift. The reason I couldn't just figure it out (despite some previous successes) was that things had changed.

I'd always had a mentor to provide feedback on my proposals and to help boost the proposals' chances of getting funded. Once I was an assistant professor, I mistakenly believed that I no longer needed a mentor, and felt that I had to go it alone.

Around the same time, the grant funding environment became more competitive. Facing these two strikes, I had that nasty string of failures.

I wasn't blind to the problem at that point. I realized that I needed to learn how to improve my grant writing. I also needed to modify the scientific approach that I was using, and make the proposals more "sellable."

I also had to discern between desirable and undesirable projects. It wasn't just about how I wrote my grant proposals, but also the very work that I was proposing. I realized that those two factors are inseparable.

My main goal with this book is to give you a shortcut, so that you can reduce the pain and misery that comes with repeated grant rejection. I want you to spend more time on more important goals -- whether they involve science, nonprofit work, or getting a grant for your business -- and less time honing your grant writing process.

What is a great (and successful) grant proposal?

A great proposal is one that results in funding that supports the proposed project. It is that simple!

There is much mythology over <u>how</u> to achieve this. There are even a few books that delve into the issue in some depth.

What few people discuss is a simple principle: getting a grant funded is about convincing someone else to <u>open up their wallet/ pocketbook/checkbook and give you money.</u>

A popular (and true) saying in the business world goes something like this:

"One of the most difficult things to get the human animal to do is open up his wallet and part with his money."

Because of this, businesspeople have studied the psychology of marketing and sales for as long as they have been doing business. Some have it figured out, others haven't.

Most poor folks writing grants are, by comparison, stuck in the stone ages. There are rumors and myths about what works and why, but through it all one simple fact is ignored: getting someone to give you money requires a positive mental response to your proposal.

Viewed this way, the premise of writing a successful grant is greatly simplified: it consists of promoting a favorable psychological response in the recipient. Nothing more, nothing less. We're not talking about trickery or deception, but we are talking about making your project as appealing as possible.

But how do we do that?

What not to do

I'll start with what <u>not</u> to do. The ways to promote an unfavorable response from a typical reviewer include:

» Presenting dense, overly technical descriptions that bore the reader, or make him lose interest

» Leaving out the "big picture" of **Why** the proposal is important

» Being condescending to the reader because you think you are better, or that you have more expertise/experience than her

» Lacking logic and consistency in your proposal

» Showing no reasonable plan for how the money will be used

» Not stating a clear problem that the funding will help you solve

Many of the failed grant proposals I've seen as a reviewer on NIH and NSF review panels are rejected for one or more of these issues. Many proposals I've seen have included all of the issues.

While a proposal with just a few of these flaws may get funded, its chances are diminished by each of those issues.

"Every proposal starts with a great idea backed up by credible person(s) and organization(s)."

In scientific grant writing circles, the person who is doing the best science is often thought to be the "game winner." In reality, this isn't necessarily the case.

Having a great project in mind -- be it scientific, business, or nonprofit -- is a starting point, but it is *only the foundation, and not the house.* The house is the effective presentation of that project in a way that promotes a favorable reaction in the reviewer.

This book is not about how to build the foundation. I will save that for another time. This book is about what to do once you have established a great foundation. It will help you maximize your chances of getting your next grant funded on the first try.

Persuasion, not manipulation

We covered what not to do, and now we'll cover what you must do to get your next grant proposal funded: persuade your reviewer that your project is **the greatest thing they've come across in the last six months.** And I'm serious about that.

You can't take a skunky idea, wrap it up in nice clothes and "sell" it to people. Even if that strategy works for the short term, it will definitely catch up with you in the long term.

Yet, on the flip side, you can have the greatest idea since mouse traps and sliced bread, but not be able to get grant funding to support its further development.

"Evoking no emotion at all is better than making your reviewer angry at you for being condescending, ripping off someone else's ideas, being manipulative, or being tedious and pedantic."

Many times this is simply because you lack persuasion and influence in your grant proposal.

This book addresses that situation and helps you "sell" your great idea. Every proposal starts with a great idea backed up by credible person(s) and organization(s). Your job is to convey that good idea, and that credibility, in an effective and *persuasive* way.

Your reader has to get excited and enthusiastic, almost to the point of jumping up and down.

Why am I using emotional words here?

Because people remember *emotions*.

Think back over the past week of your life. What stands out, and why?

In all probability, the **things that stood out the most had the most emotion associated with them**.

And unfortunately, the things associated with negative emotions usually stand out more than the positive experiences.

Our brains are wired that way. It's a survival mechanism. After all, if we did something foolish and wound up being chased by a tiger, assuming we survived, our brains would go into overdrive trying to figure out what happened, and how to prevent it from recurring.

Try to avoid invoking negative emotions. No emotion at all is better than making your reviewer angry at you for being condescending, ripping off someone else's ideas, being manipulative, or being tedious and pedantic.

However, usually "evoking no emotion" is not enough to get funding in a competitive environment.

The review process: comparing apples to apples

Most grants are reviewed in a competitive environment. A reviewer will usually look at multiple grants first, with all proposals received by the organization then considered together during one session where all reviewers are present. These meetings can span several days. Because reviewers are stuck in a room for a few days together, listening to one review after another, a great deal of boredom and creeping annoyance is present. That's why it is so important for your proposal to be easy to read and enjoyable. Make it a breath of fresh air.

Because of this review process, the proposal you submit is almost always going to be compared to the other proposals. Only the most **favorably memorable** proposals will make reviewers advocate for funding.

And that's usually what it takes to get your grant funded: getting one or more of your reviewers onboard as strong advocates.

Think about it this way: If you read a boring, unexciting proposal, would you be willing to stand up in front of a group of your peers to advocate for its funding? It's highly unlikely, right?

To be willing to stand up in front of that group of people, you'd really have to get behind that proposal and think it was something special.

And that's where influence and persuasion come in.

Learning about influence from Ernie and his diapers

I recently had the joy of helping some kids go through potty training. Potty training a 2-year-old toddler is an exercise in influence. Even a 2-year-old is independent enough to <u>not</u> listen when someone says "Use the potty, or else!" It turns out that potty training requires the same subtlety one would use to convince an adult to do something.

This philosophy holds true, even when you're telling someone to do something that will end up in a win-win result. A potty-trained toddler is more independent, doesn't have to walk around in wet or stinky diapers, and consumes less of his parents' time. It is for everyone's good. So why doesn't a toddler just immediately want to go for it? Because he is set in his ways and resistant to change.

We might look at this example and say, "A 2-year-old doesn't know any better." But adults suffer from the same kinds of problems. We simply don't know any better.

In the case of the diaper training, we happened to have a book about Ernie the Muppet, and how he was becoming a big boy by using the potty. This book used influence by example and storytelling to achieve a good end: getting other toddlers potty trained.

This "learn by example" goes much further in influencing a toddler than the direct approach does (saying "use the potty now!" in a commanding voice just doesn't cut it). At two years old, toddlers have already developed resistance to being told directly what to do, and it requires subtle influence to get them coming along.

> *"When you write a grant, you are trying to sell your ideas to your reviewer - and your reviewer knows it!"*

Now let's think about how this relates to getting grants. Your reviewers will exhibit **that same kind of mental resistance** to any idea you put forth! I'm not saying that reviewers are like two year olds, but what I am saying is that resistance to "selling" of ideas comes very early on and persists throughout life.

Every human is wired to resist or be skeptical of new ideas that come from someone else. And here's the important part for grant writing: that part of the brain becomes particularly active when any kind of "selling" is going on. Our BS detectors are on high alert!

When you write a grant, you are trying to sell your ideas to your reviewer, and that reviewer knows it!

Hence, the reviewer is in full-on resistance mode. Even if your project is going to do some good for the world (if not, you might want to reconsider the project you are undertaking), there will still be conflict between the reviewer's resistant and the project's potential good.

Yet you and your reviewer probably want the same thing in the end: the wise use of available grant money to move your field of work or business forward. Hence, it is far more effective to view this as a partnership, rather than a conflict.

The only way to accomplish this balance is to use gentle influence and persuasion (much like the Ernie potty-training book did), to convince the reviewer that you have something beneficial to offer.

My goal in talking about the Ernie book is not to equate grant writing with potty training, because they are quite different activities. However, the anecdote highlights how deep-seated the psychology you're dealing with is, and how it develops early on in our childhood. Overcoming it is the biggest challenge you'll face in getting your grant funded.

Using marketing concepts to persuade your reviewer

The marketing field has studied this kind of influence and persuasion extensively.

Whenever I bring up the subject of "marketing," a lot of the non-business types flinch.

In those circles, marketing is a *dirty word*, but it shouldn't be.

Marketing is a neutral word. It is simply about offering a product on the market in a way that connects with a buyer.

In some cases marketing can be used for good. By getting people fit, for example, health clubs do a social good. But a gym without any marketing will close its doors pretty quickly. The lack of revenue would kill it.

In some cases marketing can be used for nefarious purposes. That's why marketing has a bad name.

Let's assume that your grant proposal is focused on doing good in the world. If this is the case, you'll maximize your chances of success if you enlist the concept of "marketing."

In doing so, you'll face the same challenges that an effective marketer deals with. You are offering your "product" (your idea) on the marketplace for consideration within the set of all grants being evaluated for funding.

The challenge will be figuring out how to overcome the resistance we just discussed in order to convince someone to do something that will be good for them (in this case, funding your grant).

Here's an important side note: Part of writing a great grant proposal is figuring out "How" to do something useful for the world with your work. The concepts and ideas presented here are only useful once you already have an idea of "How" you're going to do something beneficial and useful in the world with your project.

How to apply marketing psychology to get your next grant funded

We don't learn this stuff in school. In fact, in college and high school, most people suffer through virtually endless, long, boring essay-writing assignments.

People are rarely taught how to use this simple set of communication steps to positively influence the reader. Some people may stumble upon it by chance, but it is rarely by design.

Those who study marketing psychology know how to put this to work. The rest of us need just the right combination of experiences and skills (or a book like this one!) to come up with an effective way of applying these principles on one's own.

THE PROCESS OF USING MARKETING TO GET YOUR GRANT FUNDED BOILS DOWN TO A FEW SIMPLE ACTIONS YOU CAN IMPLEMENT:

1. Grab the prospect's attention

2. Hold that prospect's attention for long enough to explain the benefits of what you have to offer

3. Explain how those benefits will be delivered

4. Assure the prospect that you have the capability/reliability to deliver the benefits

5. Explain the cost of those benefits.

6. Seal the deal.

7. That's it.

Sounds easy, right?

CHAPTER 3
How a bike shop teaches the value of marketing in your proposal

I learned the value of solid marketing when I co-founded a bicycle shop a few years ago. My goal was to get more people riding bikes instead of driving their cars due to problems associated with our dependency on oil.

My first, novice marketing message went something like this:

"Get an electric bike to save the environment and reduce dependency on foreign oil."

Now, when I say it like that, you may be thinking, "Why should I care?"

I was inexperienced, so I used this rudimentary approach right out of the gate. The marketing was about our mission (the one I stated above), rather than on the customer's mission. Needless to say, we didn't sell many bikes.

Unfortunately, my bike advertising approach is the same as most grant writers' approach grant writing! **If you approach it that way, you will always struggle at getting funded.** You may have occasional wins, but those successes will be interspersed with frequent rejections, where your reviewer just "doesn't get it."

Back to the bike shop. Many thousands of dollars in debt later, I realized the error of my ways. I took some crash courses in marketing. It turns out there's a lot of knowledge out there about how to do this, without relying on trial and error and random brilliant insights.

What if I told you this: "I have a way that you can lose fat, save money, and save your environment in only 30 minutes a day, all without the excruciating pain and boredom of having to run on a treadmill."

Maybe that got your attention. I'm talking about the same product discussed above (the bikes), but the message is transformed through the marketing lens. The revised message looks at bike selling through the lens of a customers (and the benefits they will accrue) rather than focusing on my own goals (which the customers couldn't care less about).

We are constantly bombarded by information, but not much of it is exciting. But someone who wants to lose weight sees the message above, and their attention is piqued. They begin wondering: How can I do that? Tell me more...

Take this message to heart in your grant writing. You need to present something that gets people interested from the first word - and *keeps* them interested.

Your reviewer IS your customer

The organizations and the reviewers that you send your proposals to *are your customers*. You have to *sell them* on your solution.

When writing, consider their goals, not yours.

For example, let's say you're a scientist who wants to study HIV. If you apply for a grant from an organization that wants to solve the world's energy problems, you're unlikely to succeed. You're not focusing on a problem that your customer cares about.

But if you submit it to, say, The National Institute for Allergy and Infectious Disease (part of the National Institutes of Health), and if you have a credible story for how to move the ball forward in curing HIV, you may have a shot. You have something to offer that your particular customer wants.

So, before we even get started on the four steps, you must have a product that your customer wants. Read the documents and instructions carefully to find out exactly what they want. Make sure you fit that description.

You can have a great "product" (the thing that you propose to do), and you can have great "marketing" for that product (i.e., a persuasive proposal), but if it is not the right product for your customer, none of that will matter.

How can you avoid this challenge? It's simple: make sure your customer wants your product. Read the documents and instructions carefully about exactly what they want. Make sure you fit that description.

Next, pick up the phone and talk to a live human being about your project. Ask them if they're interested. Often times, they'll give you suggestions for how to improve your idea, and how to make it more interesting for them. Listen to those ideas, and do what they say!

I hate to have to remind you of this, but I'm going to anyway: follow instructions. If your granting agency says that your proposal is limited to 10 pages max, and you submit 10.5 pages of text, it is likely your grant won't even be considered. It will be rejected out of hand. It is amazing how many people don't follow this simple step.

"Follow instructions. If your granting agency says that your proposal is limited to 10 pages max, and you submit 10.5 pages, it is likely your grant won't even be considered."

Read the instructions before you start writing, and then read them again as you get partway through. Make sure you're not just wasting your time. **Do what they ask you to do, and how they ask you to do it.**

Then, use the four-step process of persuasion to make it all come together. Read on for more information about this process.

What is a marketer's mindset?

Marketers do one thing and they do it very well. They see things from the prospect's/customer's/reviewer's point of view.

They lose their own ego, interests and desires, and they focus on the customer's wants and desires.

If this is new for you, it may seem like an arduous task. In some ways it is, because we're often taught to think only of ourselves. If we're not used to doing it, thinking like someone else can be difficult.

Just think of yourself as the customer. Drop your preexisting notions, and view your work, your product and/or your proposal from the perspective of, "What if I was coming to this for the first time, how would I respond?"

Then, figure out how to fix it to gain an improved response, and how to make it more appealing.

Your reviewers have a stack of grants to read, and they probably aren't all that excited about the task ahead of them. It takes a lot of time, and the work can be tedious.

But the grant writer who produces an interesting grant that is enjoyable to read has a big leg up. How do you make

"You must make sure that you have a product that your customer will want. Read the documents and instructions carefully about exactly what they want. Make sure you fit that description."

it interesting and enjoyable? By getting into their prospect's (reviewer's) shoes.

Reviewers are people like you and me. They have a set of needs , that may include the desire to make the world a better place, solve a particular problem (e.g. cancer, poverty, etc), curiosity, and a desire to see problems solved. Be empathetic to your reader's wants, and you will always fare better in any grant reviewing process (and in any marketing effort).

Adopt a marketer's mindset

To write effective grants, you must get into a marketer's mindset. You may have a lot of notions about what that mindset is, but it's important to understand that marketing itself is a neutral process. It can be used for good or bad. It is the process of connecting a prospect with an item.

Take tobacco and smoking, for example. The popularity of cigarettes among women in the USA began due to some very clever marketers who managed to associate smoking with women's liberation in the 1920's and 30's.[1] The association was made between cigarettes and freedom, liberation, and control of one's own destiny.

Hence, women bought cigarettes in droves in order to express their freedom and liberation. It also became a matter of solidarity with other women.

This is a genius feat of marketing that has had very unfortunate consequences.

---

1   *Tob Control 2000;9:3-8 doi:*
http://tobaccocontrol.bmj.com/content/9/1/3.extract

However, let's consider the decrease in cigarette use in the USA over the past 20 years. While it has been a multifaceted campaign, one of its most effective aspects has been making smoking seem "uncool." Hip, with it, and cool people don't smoke, according to the marketing sponsored by the government.

That marketing message may save hundreds of thousands of lives and save millions of taxpayer dollars.

Good or bad, without marketing there would be no commerce and no grants (at least not within our current economic structure).

In order to write effective grant proposals, you have to consciously adopt a marketing mentality. Most grant proposals do good for the world by addressing some pressing need or solving some problem. However, the problem isn't going to get solved, and the need will go unfulfilled, if the grant funding doesn't come through.

Why am I harping on this point? Because I've encountered many people who think that all marketing is "evil," and want nothing to do with it. I was once one of those individuals, and it's probably one of the reasons I struggled with funding. To be an effective grant writer, you really do need to understand this mindset. The first step to understanding is realizing that marketing is not always a bad thing.

SECTION 2:

THE STRUCTURE OF PERSUASION

CHAPTER 4

The structure of a reviewer's mental response

A fractal is a mathematical construct that is self-repeating at different scales[2].

For example, the California coastline from a jet airplane looks pretty jagged. If you look at a smaller section of it from a helicopter, it still looks similarly jagged. If you look at it from 10 feet up (say from a small cliff), it still looks similarly jagged. If you zoom in with a magnifying glass, it's still going to look … jagged.

A proposal has a similar fractal structure. There is an overall structure, usually comprised of distinct, labeled sections. Within each section there exists a structure that resembles the top level structure. Drilling down, each paragraph and sentence also has a structure.

We'll focus mainly on the top-level structure of your proposal in this book, but it's also important to realize that each of the principles will be used throughout your proposal in a fractal-like way.

---

2   *Benoit Mandelbrot, <u>The Fractal Geometry of Nature</u>, 1982*

At the top level, a typical proposal comprises:

1. An abstract and/or project summary of up to one page in length that summarizes the entire project.

Figure 1 - Example of the same fractal set, shown at two different scales

2. An introduction and/or background section that tells the reader where this proposal fits into the world.

3. Sometimes there is a "prior work" or "progress report" section for any ongoing work for which you're requesting continued funding.

4. A section describing the work to be done, and how it will be done.

5. Usually a separate section containing the credentials of the applicants (i.e. their CVs or resumes).

Most proposals will follow this structure, but if you want your proposal to pay off - and to get your reviewer truly enthusiastic - then you have to pay attention to a different structure.

Structure of the mental response to your proposal

As we discussed, your proposal is a selling process. Humans are resistant to being "sold," and hence you must pay careful attention to the structure of your selling approach.

It is a step-by-step response, and if you approach it out of order, then you are going to get a non-response at best, and a frustrated response at worst.

This is like a ratchet. You must do the steps in order, with each one building on the last. If you present the last one first, then it is almost as if you didn't present it at all.

Say you walk into a store and are told that you have to pay $10 as a "deposit" for your shopping trip. How would you respond? The example sounds ridiculous, right? That's because it is. The store is clearly doing things out of order. The <u>payment comes last</u>, and in no other order within our current societal context. A grant proposal works the same way. Putting the wrong thing first is akin to being asked for your money <u>before</u> you have selected something to purchase. Next we will review what those steps are.

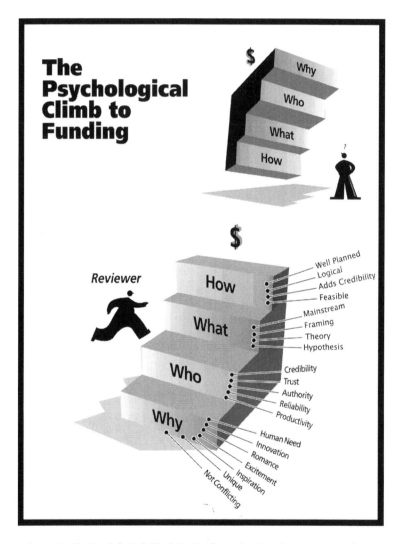

Figure 2 - The Psychological Climb To Funding - the Four Steps you must take to persuade your reviewer (bottom) and what happens if you reverse them or put them out of order (top panel).

The four sequential steps to a funded proposal

There are four steps that every effective grant proposal must take, in order, to persuade a reviewer to consider funding it.

They are:

1. **"Why"**: Why is the proposal of interest to the reviewer, agency, and world?

2. **"Who"**: Who is proposing to do the work, and are you credible?

3. **"What"**: What is the theory/model/hypothesis behind what you are proposing to do?

4. **"How"**: How are you proposing to apply the money to do it?

Those are the four steps, and they are illustrated in Figure 2.

To get the dollars - and to get the reviewer to "buy" your proposal - he or she must reach the very top, where the dollar sign is.

Without a rope or other assistive device, there's only one way they're going to get there: by climbing the steps.

That first step is Why. While you might find the occasional person who doesn't need to know "Why," she should spend hundreds of thousands or even millions of dollars on your proposed project, such people are rare.

When it comes to cracking open the checkbook, nearly anyone wants a good reason for <u>Why</u> they should do so.

Usually, the Why comes from addressing some human need or solving a human problem. There's more detail on that in the chapter on "Why."

Once you've convinced the reviewer of a legitimate "Why," the next step in the process is "Who."

In this instance, "Who" refers to you. Are you believable? Are you capable of carrying out the work? Can they trust you with their money? No matter how great the reason (the Why) you have, if the funder doesn't trust that you can do the work, you won't get the check. You have to be someone who is clearly capable of the proposed project.

Let's say you're a college freshman who is sending a proposal to the U.S. Department of Energy to develop a new type of fusion reactor that produces clean electricity. Your "Why" is quite solid: the need to develop new, clean sources of energy. But your "Who" may be lacking. You would have to jump over a very big wall to convince a reviewer that you are a college freshman who is really capable of building a fusion reactor.

Now, you may wonder, why "Why" comes before "Who" in the series of steps. Let's say you're a Nobel prize winning biologist. You've got the "Who" licked; you are clearly credible. But you're proposing to study how Peloponnesian history influenced the Greek tragedies. And you're sending this proposal to the U.S. National Science Foundation.

Well, despite your fame, they're not going to fund the work. The "Why" is not there. It is always the first step, coming before Who.

Only once you've successfully caused excitement in your reader with a good **Why**, can you convince him that you are credible.

But we still have a few steps to go.

Next comes the "What." **What** is the general theory behind your project or idea. The reviewer needs to be informed of that theory, so that she can make a sound decision.

Consider the HIV theory of AIDS, for example. The human immunodeficiency virus infects cells like macrophages, causing disfunction of the immune system and immune suppression, leading to what we call autoimmune deficiency syndrome. When explaining complex subjects like this, you must give the reviewer enough background.

Get them on the same page as you, and do it before you move onto the next step.

Remember that you can't cover this step before the preceding two steps. If you try to describe the "What" before the "Why," your readers won't be motivated to continue reading. This would be akin to sitting through the driest, most boring lecture ever. There will be no sense of "Why," and your reviewer will be left wondering, "Why am I sitting here subjecting myself to this boredom?"

When you bore the reader, your chances of getting grant funding are cut in half. They stop paying attention. Yes, they may read the words, but they are reading them only to support a conclusion they've already made: that your proposal is boring and uninteresting. That is akin to death for your proposal. And putting the What before the Why is the easiest way to kill your chances.

Put What before the Who and you'll have a similarly insidious effect on your reader's psychology. They won't know whether to trust anything that you write! All that convincing will go down the drain if they don't know that you're a trustworthy person.

If you show that you're credible <u>before</u> you start writing about the theory - say you're a recognized expert in HIV research - the reader will be much more likely to take your theoretical explanation (your What) seriously.

Let's say you're reading a short theoretical description of the HIV theory of AIDS written by a Nobel prize winner in the field. Are you likely to pay attention, and take the description seriously?

But what if the same description was scribed by a high school biology student? Will you take it as seriously? Probably not. You're likely to look for flaws or holes in their argument. Since very few writings are truly without holes (no matter who writes them), you'll find the flaws. The key is providing enough credibility so the reader is not looking for every possible flaw.

Finally, there's one more step: How.

How is simply the proposed procedure, or recipe if you will, for your project. It describes where the money will go and how it will be spent to produce the desired end result.

The "How" is a vital part of any proposal, and its importance shouldn't be diminished just because it's at the at the end of the chain (or top of the stairs, as in the figure).

Unfortunately, **most novice grant writers (and some experienced ones) focus too much on the "How," to the exclusion of the previous three steps.** That's one of the biggest reasons for grant proposal rejection.

"How" is an equal partner in ultimately convincing the reviewer, but it is <u>the last link in the chain, not the first</u>. We can't start describing a cure for HIV before we describe the cure's importance, just like you wouldn't start making a birthday cake if there wasn't a birthday coming up. The Why, Who, and What always precede the How.

CHAPTER 5

Your ratchet to success

Inexperienced grant writers usually focus on the "What and How" to the exclusion of the "Why." Then, when they get a rejection letter, they complain that, "The reviewer just didn't 'get it.' It's almost as if they didn't read the proposal! They must be ignorant!"

> *"...most novice grant writers (and some experienced ones) focus too much on the "How," to the exclusion of the other three steps that come before."*

As we discussed previously, you should change your grant writing, not blame the reviewer. The best way to do this is by understanding that if you don't successfully complete each step before you move onto the next one, the reviewer isn't going to follow you. They will keep reading, but once you've lost them mentally, their reason for reading changes to justifying a rejection.

Consider this popular marketing saying: "The difference between lettuce and garbage is the timing"

As the quote indicates, the specific order of steps is critical. So critical, in fact, that we're going to dive a bit more deeply into this issue.

A significant fraction of failed grant proposals are plagued by one of two problems:

1. One of the Why/Who/What/How is missing, or is weak.

2. These concepts are presented out of order.

I'll illustrate this for you. Let's say you're shopping for a new car (or, better yet, a new bike). You go to the dealer, and a salesperson walk up to you, sales contract in hand, asking you to look it over, sign it, and cut them the check. Then, if by some miracle you're still at the dealer after that, he offers to show you around and take you for a test drive.

Think for just a moment about what your reaction would be.

If you're like most people, you'd never get to the test drive! That's because you were presented with the "How" (i.e. you give them a check for $1,473 dollars to seal the deal) before you were presented with the Why (picking a particular style/model/price point of car), Who (reputable dealer), or What (a determination of what specific features you want, based on your usage).

Take the steps out of order and you'll be left scratching your head, wondering what went wrong, just like your salesperson.

Your proposal determines the work you will do

If you're like many people, when you read the prior section that focused on two common points of failure, you may have thought to yourself: "But wait, isn't a major cause of failure that the work proposed wasn't that great or interesting to begin with?"

The answer is yes. However, great marketing begins with a great product, and a great product addresses a compelling "Why." Let's revisit the bike dealer scenario.

Say you walk into a shop where all of the bikes are used, rundown, and rusty. Will any amount of marketing convince you to buy one of them? Probably not...

The dealer must have something that you might want, *before they can even begin marketing it to you*. A great product is a prerequisite to the marketing and sales process.

At first glance, you might find these revelations somewhat depressing. You might think to yourself, "But wait, I really do want to study the mating habits of the common American toad AND I want to get my next million dollar grant proposal to fund it."

It's important that you understand that these two goals are incompatible. You're not going to find a funder who is willing to spend that kind of money to know more about the common toad's mating habits.[3]

If you're in this boat, take a moment to console yourself, and move on.

You're not alone. Business owners and managers grapple with similar problems all the time. An aspiring entrepreneur will come up with some "brilliant" idea for a new product. (Say it's a foldable lawn chair that can convert into a portable table.) The inventor thinks, "This is so totally awesome, everyone is going to want one!"

Do you want one? I sure don't. It doesn't solve a problem for me. And I've got plenty of other junk around my house, so to add more would be ridiculous. When shopping, my criterion is that the product or service must solve a problem for me. If it doesn't, I walk away.

---

3   *It may be possible to get a small grant for this subject if you can tie the study in with some clear biological mystery or problem that needs solving, and if you can find a funding agency interested in the biology of toads.*

This is one of the major reasons that 80% of all businesses fail within 10 years. They were created based on the founder's interests, rather than on defining and filling customer needs.

The same concept carries over to grant writing, where the National Institutes of Health, one of the largest granting agencies on the planet, reports that about 80% of all submitted proposals fail.

One look at the Four Step Ratchet tells us why these proposals fail: they lack a compelling Why.

So why do so many people ignore that very important step? Because defining a good Why is challenging. We'll go into that more in the next section, but for now

"Great marketing begins with a great product, and a great product addresses a compelling 'Why.'"

it's important for you to know that this is not just about word-smithing. It is about using the proposal to define what you will do and why you will do it.

If what you're trying to do doesn't fit with the ratchet's structure, and if you want to get the funding, then you'll have to change your strategy.

Change your plan around and make it into something that you can sell according to the 4-step process. Ignore these steps and you'll be wasting your time, trust me.

You may be annoyed at this. You may think that your work is so inherently great that you deserve funding, without having to do this.

I understand where you're coming from, but let's do the math. Assume everyone thinks that way (most do, so "everyone" is a good approximation for "most"). So that means everyone deserves funding, right? Therefore, we should increase the budgets of all granting agencies to fund just about every last bit of "great" work that everyone wants to do, right?

Now we'll come back to reality and deal with the notion that we are dividing up a limited resource. When it comes to divvying up a limited resource, it all boils down to persuasion. To get a grant funded, persuasion boils down to the Four Step Ratchet.

Use the process of developing your proposal to define your project, and not the other way around. Use it to make sure you are doing something relevant for your funding agency.

THE 9-PART RECIPE
FOR DEVELOPING YOUR PROJECT:

1. Come up with a general idea of what you want to do.

2. Put that idea down on paper in a one-page "specific aims" or "project summary".

3. Examine whether your one pager covers all four steps, effectively and in order: Why, Who, What, and How.

4. Modify your project until you think it does

5. Give it to colleagues for review, and ask them specifically about whether each of the four steps is clear to them (don't just give it to them and say, "please give me feedback" - their general feedback will be about grammar and etc - in other words, useless).

6. Based on the feedback, refine what you plan to do further

7. Revise the document accordingly

8. Repeat until it is crystal clear

9. Write the rest of your proposal.

In this recipe, you may notice that "write the rest of the proposal" is only one step out of nine. YES, exactly! **Most people miss this very important point.** You may think that your job is #9, and you may launch into the writing long before the *hard work* is done.

Don't ever begin writing the rest of the proposal until you've taken all the preceding actions.

If you skip actions 1-8, you will be lost on #9. You'll struggle, you won't spend enough time on this step, and your work will produce sub-par results.

Your next action: Sit down and brainstorm a one-page project summary (or specific aims for NIH proposals) following the basic outline of Why-Who-What-How. Once you're done, read on to dive more deeply into the facets of each step.

The leaky pipe: From your mind to the prospect's mind

Let's look at grant writing from the business perspective, with your reviewers as your prospects. They are coming to your store to look at your wares, and will consider whether to buy or to get out of there with their bank balances still intact.

As a grant writer, your wares are your proposed project(s). The prospect is going shopping at more than one dealer - in fact, they are likely to be shopping at least 10 different stores before making a decision. The experience you provide has to be great to justify their choice.

The route to success is clear, but why is it so difficult to navigate, you ask? The primary problem is that human communication is a limited channel. Our brains are these fabulous devices comprising billions of neurons that can maintain very complex concepts, pictures, and ideas about what we want to do and why we want to do it.

However, when we write those ideas down, that vast information has to be distilled down into a limited, one-dimensional format. Much information is lost in this "compression" process. When your reader consumes your writing, they are re-expanding what you wrote based on their own knowledge, experience, and imagination. That re-expansion is the source of all sorts of misinterpretation.

Mathematically, if we take information and perform lossy compression[4] on it, and then uncompress it, the original is never fully restored. There are too many "free parameters."

So, our decompression algorithm has to be "smart" and fill in the gaps.

Your readers are running their own decompression algorithms. But there's an additional factor for you to contend with: *imagination*. Imagination is unpredictable and fickle. Leave gaps in your proposal and you never know how the reader will fill those gaps. Maybe thoughts of their next dental appointment. Maybe thoughts of annoyance at your dense writing. Maybe a complete misinterpretation of what you're trying to do. You never know.

The only thing you can do is carefully construct your "compression" process by including a step-by-step description of how you arrived at your thinking.

This concept reminds me of the Snake River in Idaho. The river water originally comes from a very large mountainous area located in Idaho and Wyoming. It runs together and gets "compressed" down to a single river channel. Some time ago, humans decided they wanted some of that water

---

4   *Lossy compression discards some data that can never be recovered, in order to achieve greater compression ratios, such as the popular "mp3" music format. For more information see* http://en.wikipedia.org/wiki/Lossy *compression*

to grow potatoes and other crops, so they made alternative river channels to send the water over to those crops. The region's geology includes layers of volcanic rock such as basalt, and many cracks and crevices. Much of the water that goes into these manmade canals seeps through those crevices and back into the original river channel, rather than reaching its destination at the potato crop.

Writing is a lot like these leaky canals. There will always be leaks, but your job is to route the water (i.e., your words) to the best of your ability, and avoid the really big leaks. There will always be some leaks, but you must make them as tiny as possible.

The four-step process will help you do that. In fact, psychology has found that there are four styles of learning - Why, What, How, and What If I do it now? I learned this from Eben Pagan, a successful marketer of information and educational products.[5]

Each person has a mix of these learning styles, usually with one emphasized over the others. Regardless of the balance, however, each person has to finish them in order to reach the final goal, which is "apply this now." This is where someone takes knowledge they have gained, applies it in the real world, and then assesses the results. In grant writing, the "Do it now" stage is where your proposal gets the funding.

"Your job is to route the water (your words) as best you can, and avoid the really big leaks."

You may have noticed the absence of "Who." Because it is presupposed, Who is not a learning style. Much like you would want to only learn from knowledgeable teachers, the "Who" must be credible.

---

5   *Why did I learn this from a marketer? The reason he's a successful marketer is because he's always studying the topic. If you want to be successful "selling" your projects, you should be a student of marketing as well.*

What is the link between learning styles and grants? Going back to the idea of compression, your goal is to reproduce your proposed work as closely as possible in your reader's mind.

If you take an educational approach that covers all the styles, you are far more likely to accomplish that goal.

Marketing and learning are closely intertwined. Good marketing educates the prospect about the product and its benefits. That's exactly what your grant must do. Set out with the mindset that you're going to educate your reader about your "product," and make them take action by funding it.

"The concepts of marketing and learning are intertwined. Good marketing educates the prospect about the product and its benefits. Your grant needs to do exactly that. You need to set out with the mindset that you're going to educate your reader about your "product" so that they will take the action of funding it."

SECTION 3:

OVERCOMING THE FIRST HURDLE TO CONVINCING A REVIEWER

"Assume total ignorance but infinite intelligence."

- Linus Pauling

This book will help you do a better job of "selling" your ideas so that you can avoid painful rejection and get your next grant funded. It uses a four-step process of <u>Why, Who, What, and How</u>.

There is a higher-order structure to your reviewer's thinking that's not clearly reflected by the four steps. We'll touch on that now.

The reviewer is given the responsibility of making wise choices for investing taxpayer or foundation money. Most reviewers take this responsibility seriously, much like they do their own budgets. Hence, convincing them to spend grant money on your project is a lot like asking them to spend their own money on a product.

Because of this, a reviewer (along with anyone who is being "sold" on anything) is going to go through <u>**two**</u> **psychological phases** in response to the selling message:

1. **In the first stage, the reviewer is asking "what's in it for me or the agency I represent?"** This stage is vital. If there's no "what's in it for me" in your proposal (from the point of view of the reviewer and funding agency), you won't sell your idea. It will fall flat, and never recover.

   The "what's in it for me" stage can be broken down into just one of the four steps in our climb to funding: **the Why.**

   If you don't have an appropriate answer to "what's in it for me?" (the Why), the reviewer can't move onto the next stage. The Why has to come first. Once you've presented a convincing "what's in it for me" (as detailed in the chapters on "Why" below), you can move onto the second stage.

2. **In the second stage, the reviewer is asking "Can they actually deliver what they're promising?"** Here they are looking for evidence, plans, and people who can realistically pull off the "promised land" outlined in the first stage. This isn't just an arbitrary collection of facts that provide an answer to the question, but a deliberate

series of steps that convince the reviewer that you can actually do the work: Who, What, and How. Those are covered in the next section.

While you may end up putting a lot more writing into answering #2 in your proposal, don't be fooled into thinking the hard part is done. It is, in fact, the easiest part of the process. Most novice grant writers don't know this, and as a result they do not put enough thought into #1. This is a common stumbling block to getting grants funded.

Often, the "Why" is just assumed. We may have thought about it when we started, but we don't revisit too often.

Yet the reader - or reviewer - is still at the beginning of the path, wondering why you even started out in that direction. They may be thinking, "That's not such a good direction to go in, I'd rather go down a different path."

If you can't convince them to come down your path, it doesn't matter how much "great work" you are doing, or how successful you are during the second phase of the convincing process. Once they start going down that alternate path, you have lost them for good. They'll just keep going, and become more and more confused about what you're talking about, all because you didn't get them started on the right foot in the first place. This scenario is illustrated in Figure 2.

You have to remember that you are much further down the particular path than your reviewer is. You must get them to choose your path, and then to follow you far enough to be willing to give you the money.

The problem is that, by now, you've forgotten what it was like to be so far back on that path. You are tempted to throw facts and figures at the reviewer, assuming they are up there with you and that these facts and figures will be meaningful, when they aren't.

To illustrate this point, let's say you're out backpacking for two weeks. Your friend who was supposed to join you had a car breakdown, so she's starting out on the trail two days behind you. The start of the trail is somewhat confusing, with several paths going in different directions. Your friend calls your mobile phone, and asks for directions on how she can catch up with you quickly.

Now, let's say you don't really remember the start of the trail, but you do remember the past few turns you made. So you start telling your friend about the turns to make once she gets to your present section of the trail. Will it help her?

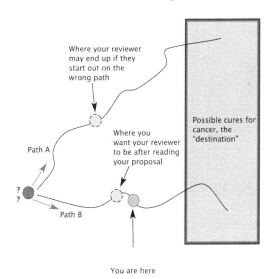

Figure 3 - Illustration of the problem you'll have
if you don't get the reviewer started on the right path with a good Why.

Not if she makes the wrong choice at the beginning due to your lack of guidance. She'll go down a completely different path, and end up far from you.

You can help her avoid that situation by thinking back to the beginning and clearly describing which path you took to get started. Then you will detail each step along the way from that beginning to where you are now. If she already knows parts of the trail, then your description may be abbreviated, but it would be foolish for you to just skip it entirely because she may get lost. That would ruin your trip, right?

This is how you have to approach grant reviewers. You have to lead them down the right path, and keep guiding them down that path all the way to the destination. The beginning of that path is Why, and then the other turns are the Who, What, and How. Because the Why is so critical, let's dive into it first.

CHAPTER 6

Why *"Why?"*

Why is Why so important to getting funding?

Funding is a scarce resource that must be apportioned. We're dealing with a fixed pool of money. Whenever there is a scarce resource, getting some of it comes down to convincing *other people* to share it.

Convincing other people comes down to persuading them. The first step of persuading them comes down to defining for them the reason <u>Why</u> you need the money.

Returning to our example of the bike dealer, the successful bike sale starts with "Why," or what purpose will the bike serve to the customer?

Without a purpose in mind, no one will buy a bike. Depending on "**Who**" they are, their purpose might be different. Some might want to use a bike for sport or exercise. Some might want a bike to save money while getting to work. Some might want a bike to thumb their noses at big oil companies.

In all cases, there's always going to be a reason "**Why**", or the sales process can't proceed. Without a reason "Why", customers will not even show up.

But your grant reviewer doesn't have a choice about whether or not to physically show up in your store (i.e., read your grant proposal). So let's modify our analogy a little bit.

Figure 4 - **Don't cause this reviewer's headache!**

Grant reviewers have enough headaches as it is, typically with 8-12 or more proposals to read within a short time span. Worse, they often have to go sit in a room with other reviewers for a day or more discussing proposals. If you make their lives harder, they aren't going to be happy with you, which means your chances of funding are lower.

Write easy-to-read text, don't use a lot of buzzwords, and explain all specialist terms.

And, most of all, help your proposal stand out from the crowd in a favorable way by making it engaging from the start, with a catchy "Why." That means a great title, and an engaging read, especially at the beginning.

Imagine that you're totally uninterested in bikes, but as part of a market research program, you've obligated yourself to visit 10 bike shops and go through a sales process at each one, while an observer (posing as a "friend") measures your response. At the end, you'll get $1,000 for participating.

In most shops, it will go something like this: You walk in and the salesperson asks the dreaded, "May I help you?" (the most generic and useless sales message, ever).

You respond, "I'm thinking about a bike." The salesperson proceeds to show you an array of several different bikes, highlighting all of the detailed features like Dura-Ace derailleurs, carbon fiber cranks, and aero spoke wheel sets (I'm using buzzwords for a reason here).

That salesperson dove immediately into the "what," before discussing "why" with you. Most do.

But then imagine going into a shop where the salesperson instead asks, "Are you looking for a bike today, or do you have a existing bike that you're looking to add to?"

After you respond that you're looking for a bike, the salesperson asks "What would you use it for?" You mumble something about riding to work on it.

He can tell that you're a newbie, and so he explains the benefits of riding a bike. He tells you about several customers who've lost over 80 pounds by riding their bikes. He tells you about all the money you can save. He tells you about how an electric bike makes it easier to ride up hills and in hot weather, and how it's a great motivational tool.

In other words, he's directly addressing the "Why" before any of the other aspects. He actually manages to get you just a little bit interested before going on to explain the benefits of each bike.

In the first example of the salesperson who never got you past "Why," the rest of the visit is mostly going to find you just pretending to listen to the pitch because you have to (you want that $1,000). You'll probably be ready to head for the exit at the first chance you get!

In the second case, you may actually enjoy listening, since you're getting something from the exchange. Do you want your reviewer bracing to head for the exit as soon as they start reading your proposal? Of course you don't.

In the second example -- with the salesperson who piqued your curiosity with a good "Why" -- you're more likely to pay attention because your interest is piqued.

The identical psychological processes come into play when a reviewer reads your grant proposal.

Pique their interest at the beginning with a good "why" and they'll keep reading with heightened interest and attention. If your "Why" is weak or absent, however, then the rest of the review process will find them sitting there, bored, much like you would be after listening to a salesman drone on and on about derailleurs, carbon fibers, headsets, and crank sets.

Which grant proposal will get the million dollars? The one with a great "Why" at the beginning, or the one that immediately launches into "What and How" (e.g. hypotheses, theories, etc)? That's right, door number one wins the prize.

"Why" is the emotional hook

We like to think of ourselves as perfectly rational decision makers. We like to think that for each decision we make, a perfectly "logical" path led us there. In reality, nothing could be further from the truth. The vast majority of our decision making takes place at an unconscious and "emotional" level. Usually, the logic comes after the decision, and justifies it in hindsight.

In fact, without emotionally-based decision making, we would be lost. There is too much information in the world. This is one of the reasons we don't have real "thinking" computers. The number of options to be explored for any decision is virtually infinite. The most logical solution is the one that optimizes all possible parameters and outcomes.

Let's consider chess as an example. In this one little game, with very limited rules for how pieces can be moved, there is a space of possible moves that is so large that no computer can search it. Programmers have made "smart" chess-playing computers by combining the machines' capacities for searching a limited subset of the space of possible moves, along with **guesses.** In computer parlance, these heuristics are little shortcuts that humans have figured out, and then coded into the computer program. That way, the computer doesn't have to consider every possible outcome (and sit there for thousands of years doing so before making a move).

This example illustrates that, even if we want to be perfectly logical, we can't. We will be permanently stuck in indecision. So, functioning people learn to make decisions based on their "gut," which is another word for heuristics and emotions. When we make a bad decision, we (hopefully) learn from that mistake and make a better decision next time.

Your grant reviewer will use a similar process. He can't possibly make a "logical" choice about which proposed project will be most likely to succeed. Remember that bit about the crystal ball? Predicting just two minutes into the future for a complex system involving humans is impossible for the most powerful computer (or human mind). With grants, we're talking about predicting months to years into the future, and the ultimate outcome of a real-world project.

Although a reviewer may use rational "sounding" words to justify a proposal review, she really has no clue whether you will succeed or not. She simply took some shortcuts to make a decision (since she had to), and then tried to justify that decision with some surface logic. If she put down on the review, "Because my gut told me these folks are going to succeed," she'd be laughed out of the room.

This is not to say that the heuristics we use as reviewers are totally wrong. We look at various factors such as the applicant's track record (see Chapter 9 on "Who"), the estimated feasibility, and so on.

But before we can estimate a project's success chances, we must answer the fundamental question: **Would we care if it did?**

That's what the Why is all about. The answer to this question involves emotions such as interest, care and excitement (not logic, initially).

This initial emotional response is exactly why your first step must be to capture your reviewer's emotional response. You have to get him or her excited about your **why**. You need to get your reviewer **caring** about your proposal <u>before</u> you try to do anything else.

If they are not excited and do not care from the start, it does not matter how good the rest of the proposal is. It is unlikely to hold sway enough to get funding. And beware, for getting this down is the hardest aspect of grant writing for most people.

Why may be "My father died of cancer and I want to solve it"

Or it may be to reduce the number of people who die from poverty.

Or it may be simply "Scientific curiosity - the drive to solve an unsolved problem"

There has to be a why. If you don't get the emotions onboard, you don't get the reviewer onboard.

Why is "Why" so hard?

The lack of a sufficient "Why" -- not only for the big picture of a grant, but for each step proposed in the project -- is one of the main deficiencies in the grant writing process. It's why most grants fail. To get your reviewer excited about your proposal, it simply has to be on your radar.

EXAMPLE OF AN EXPLORATORY PROPOSAL
(THAT FAILED)

"Our long-term goal is to integrate proteomics, genomics, and computing in a systems biology fashion to provide tools for examining and modeling microbial evolution. Herein we propose a proof-of-principle test of a novel combination of proteomic methods, applying them to the problem of determining the multiple proteomic and genomic changes that occur during adaptive evolution to offset the fitness costs of antibiotic resistance."

This is a snippet of text from the specific aims of one my grant proposals that failed to garner any reviewer interest. Even though it doesn't use the word "understanding," it is nonetheless very exploratory. It sounds like we're going on a fishing expedition to gain some knowledge, but it is not clear how we will apply that to solve problems.

Here's another snippet:

*"**The Specific Aim of this proposal** is to determine the multiple genome changes that occur during adaptive evolution compensating for the fitness costs associated with an antibiotic resistance mutation in E. coli."*

Again, this is very general and unfocused. Reviewers don't like proposals that are simply going to generate knowledge, unless the call for proposals is specifically about generating data or knowledge (e.g. for Sequencing The Human Genome, we necessarily have to generate data).

The problems shown above can't be handled with just a simple rewrite, but require a complete re-thinking of the approach. For that reason, we didn't revise this proposal for resubmission; we went in a new direction with this work. Sometimes you have to do that.

Perhaps "Why" is difficult because of our educational training. Through our high school and college undergraduate educations, we rarely are encouraged to ask "Why?" Instead, we are told to sit there and passively receive knowledge derived from other people who asked "Why?" in the past. By the time we get the knowledge, the "Why" is usually obvious in retrospect. We don't hear about the projects that failed. We don't have to justify which prospective project might be a better bet. We just don't have to think about it much because we are taught to "do," and not ask questions.

This problem extends beyond college. When we apply for a job, we're told what the requirements are. We don't have to ask "Why am I doing this?" to get a paycheck. We just have to do the assigned job. In fact, asking "why am I doing this?" might be an impediment to getting a paycheck with some employers!

It is only through activities like grant writing, or trying to sell a product to a customer, that we have to really start exercising the "Why" part of our minds.

Exercise the Why muscle, starting now

That "Why" muscle can and does grow weak with disuse. To become a better grant writer, you must **exercise it regularly**.

Exercise your "Why" muscle by <u>not</u> passively accepting information. When you read the newspaper or listen to the radio, ask yourself "Why are they telling me this? What message are they really sending?" Use similar cynicism when reading books or papers from your field. Build that muscle to the point that anytime you sit down to write a grant proposal, the "Why" is justified.

Following your curiosity and letting it lead you also helps. Curiosity is an incredibly potent motivator and developer of the "Why" muscle.

Whether you're already good at this or you need some practice, the next step will be to translate your ability to ask "Why" into the ability to clearly state the "Why" in

"If you don't get the emotions onboard, you don't get the reviewer onboard."

your proposal. When you can do that, the reviewer will buy into your proposal and get excited over it.

CHAPTER 7

How to do Why

Fill a need to engage your reviewer

Grant writing is all about filling people's needs. There are very few (if any) grants given out in the world that aren't ultimately designed to fill some human need.

"Filling a need" is not about satisfying your own curiosity or interests as the grant writer! We're talking about <u>general human needs</u>, not your own specific needs.

Engage your reviewer by making it clear from the outset what human need your work addresses. That human need tells the reviewer "Why" the grant might deserve funding.

Your job is to simply find where your own interest, curiosity, and motivation intersect with some human need.

We're talking about needs like health, food, social acceptance, recognition, curiosity about our world, social stability, and so forth.

 Unless you can figure out where your interests intersect with one of those needs, there is no reason to write your proposal. This must be clear in your mind from the outset because it determines the rest of the grant writing process.

Hone in on a need by solving a problem

You can make your proposal more effective by focusing on a stumbling block that's preventing some group from getting its needs met, and then using your project to address that challenge.

The human mind is a problem-solving machine. People like solving problems. If you make it clear that you are solving an important problem, your proposal will resonate with your reviewer. You'll get them engaged mentally in the outcome, and wanting to solve the problem with you.

Curiosity-focused versus need-based proposals

In scientific grant writing, people often submit curiosity-focused proposals, rather than problem-solving proposals. Sometimes these curiosity-focused proposals get funded, but most don't. While it is a human need, curiosity is not as basic and driving a need as, say, avoidance of cancer, or solving the world's energy problems. Most funding agencies, whether private or public, are focused on solving problems to improve human lives.[6]

Proposals that are centered on problems are far more likely to succeed than those that based on curiosity or theory.

But your proposal can't focus on any old problem. It must be something that fits with the agency's mission. Each funding agency has a specific, problem-solving mission.

For example, the U.S. National Institutes of Health (NIH), has sub-agencies that are focused on solving various types of human disease. One example is the National Cancer Institute, which is

---

6   *There are some additional nuances to the issue of curiosity in proposals that didn't make it into this edition of the book, but you can see a video on the subject at http://fourstepstofunding.com/extra*

on a mission to cure cancer. The Gates Foundation focuses most of its resources on solving third-world health issues. The list goes on...

Some funding agencies give grants to solve indirect issues. The National Human Genome Research Institute at the NIH, for example, focuses on decoding the human genome, knowing that this is one step removed from solving human problems. The organization was founded because researchers realized that without a deeper understanding of how the human genome functions, progress on disease research in all areas (e.g. cancer, heart disease, diabetes, etc.) would be limited.

Most proposals either directly address a problem, or are one step removed from it.

Often, a funding agency will put out specific "requests for proposals" or "program announcements." These are the best possible indicators of the problems your project should be addressing. If the agency has bothered to put out a specific request, that means it is serious about solving that problem.

Read these program announcements carefully, and make sure you are solving a problem that fits within the scope of what they are asking for. If your work does not fit, you have one of two choices:

1. Change the work you want to do

2. Find a different program to approach for funding

Some people might be thinking of an "option 3," which is to "spin" their work so that it fits the agency's mission. Avoid this temptation. It almost never works, and it will waste both your time and your reviewers' time.

This is not to say that you shouldn't ever modify your approach to address the funding agency's target problem. But if you think you can cover up a poor fit with some fancy word-smithing, you'll wind up in the "glass slipper" scenario (trying in vain to get that shoe to fit on anyone who comes along). Reviewers will see through your attempts, and your credibility (the Who) will wind up in the toilet.

So, your next step is to go out and look at program announcements that fall within your scope of funding interest, and figure out what problems need to be solved. Matching your capabilities with funding agency interests is the very core of a great grant proposal! **Don't skip this step, do it now!**

Value comes from problem solving, not "Understanding"

"Understanding" is a nebulous word that's overused in grant proposals, and particularly in research proposals. If I get a "better understanding" of how cells become cancerous, does that solve the problem of cancer? Maybe, but not necessarily.

Understanding is completely open-ended and analogous to the Snake River canals I discussed earlier in this book. Understanding can be interpreted in many different ways, and you can't assume that your reviewer's interpretation will go in your favor. In fact, it is best to assume that it won't.

In the big picture of your grant proposal, you will face a tough road if you are tempted to just go for "understanding." Few reviewers will get excited by "understanding." In fact, there's more than enough knowledge and data in the world already. We are flooded by it, and it grows exponentially.

The key question is: Can any of the data/knowledge/ understanding be translated into solving problems?

In the Internet era, we are subject to data and knowledge floods. Yet those deluges haven't helped solve world problems like pollution, cancer, poverty and war.

Hence, when you propose a project that adds to this flood of data, without showing *specifically* how the knowledge you generate *will be applied to solve a particular problem,* your proposal will be seen as having very little value. This isn't good because to receive funding, your grant must be viewed as valuable.

What is "value," anyway?

A major challenge grant writers face is the fact that people do not know how to value things. This means that your reviewers don't know a *priori* how to value the project you're proposing.

Considering the fact that there's already a flood of knowledge and understanding in the world, it's easy to see why more of the same is *not valued* very highly by most (except by specialists in that same narrow area of concern).

So people suffer from information overload and an inability to value projects, unless those projects are very close to their hearts. On the other hand, most people put a high value on <u>getting problems solved</u>. They put an even higher value on solving those issues that they have a personal stake in.

For example, a reviewer whose father is suffering from cancer is quite likely to see the value in a proposal that solves an important piece of the cancer puzzle, or that provides a new treatment.

"Matching your capabilities with funding agency interests is at the very core of a great grant proposal!"

Therefore, in order to have your project considered valuable, you must work on a problem, rather than just going for understanding.

That said, there are certain situations in which the word "understanding" is justified, such as when it is immediately qualified by a specific outcome that flows from the understanding.

Whenever you find yourself writing the word "understanding" in a grant proposal, look at it carefully to determine whether you've fallen into the "knowledge generation" trap, and if so, change it.

Fill a Gap, Cross a Hurdle: Unleashing the creative problem solver

The "problem solving" paradigm is so important to a good Why that we're going to visit it from another angle to make sure that this message really sinks in.

Let's say you're doing poverty research, and you're wondering, "How can I find a suitable problem to solve in a proposal?"

The answer is simple. Look at what roadblocks are keeping our interest area from moving forward right now. This is called "identifying the Gap" or "identifying the Hurdle."

I got this notion from one of my mentors, Marshall Edgell. He teaches a grant writing class for graduate students that focuses on the development of Gap-filling proposals.

The Gap is simply the difference between where your field/area is now, versus where it could be in a more ideal future.

Framing your grant proposal in terms of "the Gap" is powerful, because it focuses your thinking and gives you a problem-solving-based proposal.

In the case of poverty, the Gap may be that more and more people are falling into financial despair, despite current attempts to address the problem. The Gap applies to almost anything; it doesn't matter what area you're writing a grant proposal for. It may be cancer, poverty, energy, transportation, women's health or racism, to name just a few. In each case, we much overcome the Gap to get to where we want to be.

This approach can also be difficult because, in order to identify the Gap, you must delineate a "future vision" of where you think the field could be or should be. Overcoming the Gap will take us a step closer to that vision. Developing that future vision isn't always easy because it comes from our right brain, rather than our left. It is not something you can derive through logical, conscious analysis. Yet we are trained by school systems to mostly focus on precise, stepwise, logical analysis. You won't get a potent future vision out of that kind of thinking.

The "future vision" aspect of Gap identification can only be undertaken by quieting the logical, conscious mind, and allowing the creative mind to step in and come up with ideas.

Creative innovators use various methods to achieve this more open state of mind. Things you may try include:

1. Take frequent, short cat naps during the day, in which you allow yourself to just daydream for up to 20 minutes at a stretch. Both Thomas Edison and Albert Einstein did this, and so should you! Just don't allow it to go on long enough to fall into a deep sleep.

2. Go for a walk, and focus on the present moment rather than all of your current pressures or past events. Just look at your local environment and "be present." It is amazing how well our creativity functions when we just relax and appreciate the present moment.

3. Practice short bits of meditation where you visualize the future, without criticizing what comes to you. Save the criticism for later.

The topic of harnessing your creativity is vital, but it goes beyond the scope of this book. However, I strongly recommend that you try the above methods and/or do other research and reading into how to enhance your creativity. Once the creativity begins flowing it will be easy to picture how "things could be," and to use that image to define what stands between you and your future vision.

These exercises can help reveal a "Gap" between where the field is now, and where it could be in an improved future. Focus all of your effort on methods and approaches to fill that Gap, and you will have a great proposal.

Innovation is a potent "why"

Human beings are curious. In fact, our curiosity is a potent force that accounts for much of our progress and development, and it is something that differentiates us from animals. Part of curiosity is the desire for newness and novelty. It comes from enjoying change and difference, rather than settling for the same. This is why, in many grants, being seen as "innovative" pushes the reviewer's novelty and curiosity buttons. It will likely get them them excited, enthusiastic and more involved.

There's a common saying, "There's nothing new under the sun." In many ways that is true. Humans are acting out the same patterns that they have for tens of thousands of years. Most core ideas we have about our lives, ourselves, or our universe are not new or unique.

So how can we reconcile these two distinct concepts -- the notion that there's nothing new versus the need to be innovative?

This is exactly why a lot of grant writers struggle with innovation. They wonder, "How can I be innovative if nothing is new?"

It's not that difficult. Being innovative is not about inventing a whole new approach or technology. It is simply about *solving problems in new ways.* The "Lifestraw" is an excellent example of this. It's a light, portable, water filtering device used to get safe drinking water by residents of impoverished areas.

This straw applies an old concept in a new way. Water filters have been around for decades. The problems with contaminated water have existed in impoverished areas for years. Straws have been around at least since 1888, when they were patented by Marvin Stone. The Lifestraw just combines the two concepts and uses them to make headway on a particular human need in a new and more efficient way.

EXAMPLE FROM A PROPOSAL WITH A CLEAR GAP
(THAT WAS FUNDED)

*"In 2003, the National Human Genome Research Institute (NHGRI) launched a pilot project called Encyclopedia Of DNA Elements (ENCODE), in order to identify functional elements in the human genome sequence. The pilot phase rigorously analyzed a defined portion (44 defined euchromatic regions approximating ~1% of DNA sequence) of the human genome sequence and investigated the genesis of the transcripts in great detail(1). The pilot phase confirmed pervasive intragenic and intergenic transcription, painting a picture of significant complexity, including alternative splicing, new exons, and overlapping transcripts. Redundancy of transcription was observed in multiple tissue types, and many of the observed transcripts did not resemble known protein-coding transcripts, nor did they appear to be functional non-coding RNAs. **These transcripts remain unannotated, and their biological relevance remains unanswered.** A key method to producing insight into the nature and relevance of a transcript is to determine experimentally whether and when they are translated into proteins."*

I've boldfaced the critical part here, which is the GAP. Here we have biology doing a bunch of very complicated stuff, and nobody knows why. The GAP is highlighting that problem that remains to be solved, and is then followed by details about how we are going to address it:

"A key method to produce insight into the nature and relevance of a transcript is to determine experimentally whether and when they are translated into proteins. This can be done using high throughput mass-spectrometry to analyze expressed proteins, mapping the results using software to determine the encoding locus on a genome, a process known as "proteogenomic mapping" (2).....The goal of this project is to use the latest mass spectrometry technologies to produce large-scale proteogenomic data sets .... that can be used in conjunction with transcript analyses to improve functional annotation of the proteins and splice variants produced by those transcripts.

As you can see, innovation isn't about inventing a whole new technology. It is simply about solving problems with more efficient or effective solutions. These solutions often tackle a problem from a different angle than anyone has thought of before.

To flex your innovation muscle, practice brainstorming. Try this: take a problem that you are working on, and develop a quick mind map for it. Write the problem down in the center of a page, and for 10 minutes do free association of concepts and ideas that relate to the central problem. Do not censor yourself; no matter how "silly" the idea is, write it down! The reason innovation is so hard for many of us to achieve is because we censor ideas before they ever get a chance (that's our inner critic at work).

To be innovative, it is important to practice silencing the inner critic through exercises like brainstorming.

A great title conveys "Why," so that your reader wants more

What part of your grant will the reviewer see first? The title, and then the applicant's name. This is the first opportunity to get them excited, or to get them bored, about your grant proposal.

Here's an amazing "fact" from the world of sales: Changes in headlines on a sales letter or advertisement can account for more than four- to fivefold differences in the number of sales. Compared to a headline, the ad text accounts for only about 30% of the power. The headline is the first chance to get your prospect (reviewer) wanting to dive in and to read more.

Newspapers and magazines, as well as bestselling authors, are masters at creating great titles that draw in their readers. Take this headline from USA Today for example:

> "20 Things You Should Never Buy Used"

That is a hard one to resist. Just seeing that headline makes me want to dive in and find out more.

But what if that headline had been:

> "Buying used electronic goods can be problematic"

That's okay, but is it nearly as compelling? Do you want to dive in and read it?

The first step in "Why" is convincing your reader <u>Why they should want to dive in enthusiastically and read your proposal</u>.

The process is simple (see example on next page):

1. Put your title first (never last).

2. Brainstorm at least 20 versions of your title <u>on paper</u>. Be whimsical, and don't limit yourself. Focus the brainstorms around your human needs fulfillment, problem solving, and innovation. Don't censor yourself if other stuff comes out; just keep going.

3. Select the top three brainstorms. These will be ones that arouse curiosity, intrigue, excitement, and so forth. Run them by friends or colleagues for their feedback.

4. Based on the feedback you receive, iterate to see whether you can combine them or improve any of them further.

5. Remove narrow, field-specific buzzwords that a general grant reader might not understand. Replace them with terms that you're sure readers will know. Save the specifics for the "What" and "How" sections, and leave them out of the title. For example, if you work in cancer research, it might be okay to use the "buzzword" p53 (the name of a cancer-related protein) because almost everyone in the cancer research field knows what that is. But if you used the name of some other more obscure protein, like chk4, that only a handful of people know about, then it won't

EXAMPLE OF ELECTRIC BIKE HEADLINES (TITLES)

I co-own a shop that sells electric bikes to get people riding their bikes more often, which enables them to exercise and helps them lose weight. Initially we tried many standard ads with titles like:

"Electric bikes help you with hills" or,

"Electric bikes give you a boost when you need it."

Those ads were ineffective, and we got little response from them. Then I developed an ad with an engaging title. One of our most effective ads to date had the title:

"Your bike doesn't give you any exercise"

It was followed up with an explanation that most people own bikes that sit in their garage unused, and an unused bike won't provide exercise. I tied that message into how an electric bike provides more motivation to ride. The title was the most important part of this ad because it drew the reader in to find out more.

help your case. People won't be drawn in, and will likely be confused by the jargon.

6. Make sure that the final version of your title fits within the designated space (e.g. NIH proposals have strict limits on title length, presently 80 characters or about 15 words).

7. Let your title sit for a while. A few days or more is optimal.

8. Come back for more brainstorming, if necessary.

The sooner you start this brainstorming exercise, the sooner you'll have an inspiring title.

EXAMPLES OF BRAINSTORMING TITLES FOR THIS BOOK

Here are just a few of the titles that I played with in coming up with "Four Steps To Funding." I had a list of over 30, some of which were terrible, but all of which led me to a short, catchy title that conveys what the book is about. Your grant title should do the same.

» The Grant Rejection Cure

» Why What Who How

» Grants from Heaven

» The Grant Fountain

» The Simple Formula For Million Dollar Grants

» Four Pillars Of Grant Funding

» Four Steps To Grant Funding And Rejection Avoidance

» Get Your Grant Paid

You can judge a grant by its first few sentences

Your goal as a grant writer is to pull your readers forward through your text in a way that entices them to want to find out more about the project.

That's the only way to get them to really pay attention, and avoid the very common "the reviewer didn't get it" rejection.

HOW TO BRAINSTORM A GREAT OPENING FOR YOUR GRANT:

1. Use the same brainstorming technique that you did with the titles. Brainstorm at least 5-10 versions of your first few opening sentences.
2. Prioritize them according to your favorites.
3. Read them over for clarity, removing all unneeded words, buzzwords, and jargon.
4. Make sure that they are realistic and feasible with respect to the budget you will ask for and the timeframe. It is important to generate enthusiasm, but it is just as important to be realistic about what you can accomplish.
5. Let those sentences sit for a few days, before you come back to reevaluate them.
6. Resist the temptation to launch into any Who, What (theory) or How (steps). Your first few sentences are simply to engage the reader with your big picture goals so that they will keep reading to find out those other things in due time.

If you lose your reader's interest early on, he or she certainly won't get it. They'll just be reading your proposal to go through the motions, and to do their job. Nothing more, and nothing less.

The first few lines of your abstract and/or project summary are absolutely vital. Within those first few lines, you must offer a compelling and interesting "Why," or your proposal will be rejected.

The Why includes two things: Why should the reviewer keep reading, and why do you deserve funding?

In the next section we'll explore how filling human needs by solving human problems is always the most potent answer to the second question: Why you deserve funding? The first question can be answered by keeping the text concise and absent of many buzzwords, and by focusing on the "big picture" reason for Why the work is important and who will care about it. It also requires successful "compression," as discussed earlier in this book.

Since your reader sees the first few sentences of your project summary or specific aims first, you must make them compelling to draw the interest forward.

Boiling it down to a simple how-to formula for a great Why

You'll have more engaged reviewers if you follow this formula when writing your next proposal. They may still find fault in your proposal, but at least they won't be bored or disinterested. To reduce the chances of the reviewer finding other faults (and rejecting your proposal), keep reading to make sure you cover the Who, What, and How.

THERE IS A SIMPLE FORMULA FOR IMPLEMENTING A GREAT WHY:

1. Define who your target audience is (i.e. the Funding agency and its reviewers)
2. Define what human need they want to fulfill with the proposals they accept (there are scant few funding agencies that don't exist to fill some human need).
3. Define a pressing problem (or Gap) that you will solve, within their targeted human need.
4. Determine whether you will be able to convincingly implement the subsequent steps for this pressing problem (the Who, What, and How)
5. Now, step outside your head for a few moments and look at your "Why" from another point of view. Is it compelling, interesting, innovative, and solving a good problem? Get a friend or colleague to give you some feedback.
6. Make sure that you make your why very clearly at the beginning of your proposal. You will need to explain "Why" in your abstract, project summary, specific aims, executive summary, or any other "summary" sections of the proposal. Then, at the beginning of the main text, you'll need to dive into explaining this "why" in more depth before explaining anything else.

SECTION 4:
FROM CREDIBILITY
TO FUNDING

CHAPTER 8

The three steps to credibility

Once you've identified a great "Why" that gets your reviewer interested to find out more, your reviewer is going to ask, "Do I believe that these people can pull it off?"

You may be proposing a cure for cancer or poverty. Both have great, compelling "Whys." Yet a lot of people have tried to solve those problems already. Once you convince your reviewer that you're working on a worthy problem, their mind next switches into a mode of asking, "Can they pull it off?" That is all about your credibility.

You build credibility in stages. In the first stage, the reviewer asks "**Who** is it? Do they have the experience to do the work?" If you don't have the experience to accomplish your goal, your reviewer will be skeptical.

In the next stage, the reviewer asks "**What** is the theory behind this, and is it a credible theory of how the world works?" You must present a reasonable model of the world in your grant or the reviewer will get lost.

Finally, the reviewer asks "What are the steps being proposed to do the work? Are they going to lead to the promised solution?" In other words, the reviewer is asking, "**How** are they going to do the work?"

Do not start on these steps until you've pinned down your Why. These steps depend on a great "Why."

CHAPTER 9

Who are you to ask for a million dollars?

What's the difference between a painting by artist Pablo Picasso and one that a local artist in your town produces?

There may be technical differences in style, approach, and painting, but those aren't the most important differences. The big difference is the name.

If I'm an art buyer, I know that a Picasso will be worth more money - no matter *which* Picasso it is - than a painting by an unknown artist. The unknown artist may produce a work that is in fact better than any of Picasso's, but it simply does not matter in the value equation.

The same formula applies in many different situations. Pick any famous novelist, for example, and look at the cover of one of their recent books. Notice the relative size of the typeface for their name versus the name of the book.

For really famous authors, the name is often in bigger type than the title! Yet for a relatively unknown author, the title is in big type (and must be compelling!), and the name is in small type. Look at the cover of the book you're reading (no, I'm not famous yet).

Your name and your reputation are vital to convincing the reviewer that you have the credibility to do the proposed work.

I cover this topic in more depth in my upcoming book, "The Golden Ticket in Science: Funding and Recognition Through The Power of Marketing."

The bottom line is that if you have a well-known name within the field of your proposal, you will be giving a positive answer to the "can they do it?" question.

If you don't yet have a known and established name, don't despair. There are many things you can do in a proposal to boost your credibility.

Who is in "What" you do

How do famous people get that way? It's usually several factors, including:

1. Producing **great** work of some kind.

2. Doing a good job of marketing that gets their products into other people's hands.

3. Persistence.

4. Having a good PR agent (or being good at PR yourself).

5. Standing out and being different.

The first item on that list is all about what you do, and centers around the quality and excellence of the "product" that you produce.

If you are unknown, you must have a good "product" on two levels:

1. At the level of the work you're proposing to do, it must be interesting, well thought out, and innovative.

2. At the level of the grant proposal, it must be well written, logical, and focused.

Taking these two steps dramatically increases your credibility if you are an "unknown."

My father once applied for graduate school (in the days before word processors). A famous two-time Nobel prize winner was on the admission committee, and because my father made a single spelling error, his application was rejected by the Nobel Laureate.

When you are "unknown," mistakes like that can cost you more dearly than if you are "known." That's because people have no other clues to go by than what they see in front of them. If there are mistakes in what they see, and if they have no additional information, they will assume that the mistakes are a reflection of your abilities.

To gain credibility, take real care with your proposal. Make sure that it looks great, reads really well, is logically consistent, well organized, and so forth.

Give yourself enough time to accomplish this. You're not going to produce a large, complex proposal (as many scientific proposals are) in only a few days. It will require multiple iterations over a matter of weeks.

It will also require sufficient input from people who can fill in for your blind spots. You need a good proofreader, and someone who understands your field of interest well enough to give you deeper-level feedback on your proposal's logic and structure.

Ignore these steps and you'll produce a document that is hard to follow, confusing, and full of mistakes. Your credibility is likely to go into the toilet rapidly. And needless to say, you won't get the funding.

Here is a summary of the steps you can take to accomplish this goal:

1. Write your draft weeks before the proposal is due, and ask several other people review it. Be careful in your interpretation of their criticisms because if they don't like

some aspect, they may not understand why they don't like it. In an attempt to be helpful, they'll tell you what they think the problem is, but often the real problem is deeper (i.e. failure to garner excitement, lack of clarity, etc).

2. Carefully read your proposal to yourself, out loud. Reading out loud will help you spot mistakes you would not otherwise notice.

3. Stay focused on the one problem that you want to solve. Resist the temptation to go off into other, related topics. A focused proposal indicates that the writer has a focused mind; this is a vital credibility booster.

4. Follow the instructions of the granting agency. Failure to do so indicates sloppiness. You can't afford to come across as sloppy, so follow the instructions.

"Who" you are is who others say you are

Humans are social beings who rely on social cues to make many of their decisions. In his book *Influence*, Robert Cialdini talks about a case where a woman was repeatedly chased and stabbed by a man in the city, with over 20 onlookers witnessing the event from their windows. None of the onlookers called the police or did anything to stop the crime. At first, many people chalked this up to the "harsh unfriendliness and cynicism of city people." People lamented about what society was becoming.

Then a group of psychologists studied the case in depth. They formulated a hypothesis, and began testing it in other situations. They showed that the cause wasn't the cruel callousness of city dwellers, but rather that everyone who was watching the event was waiting for a cue from someone else to take action. Since nobody saw anyone else doing anything, they all figured it wasn't really an emergency (or that if it was, someone else would have called the police).

In subsequent studies, the psychologists found out that in any crowded, emergency situation, the crowd will do nothing until one person takes action and makes it clear that there is indeed an emergency! Then others take the cue and start acting.

This may seem like a digression, but it is closely related to the "Who" of your proposal. In other people's eyes, you are who people say you are. This is particularly potent in a grant-reviewing situation, where people sit around in a room going through stacks of grants, discussing them one at a time. One reviewer with something negative to say about you or your proposal can sway the whole crowd. Conversely, one reviewer who is unboundedly enthusiastic about it may be equally as infectious.

You can use this to your advantage by obtaining and highlighting "social proof" in your proposal (see the recipe on the next page).

You must market yourself to have a good "Who"

You should constantly be looking for opportunities to "market yourself." You may bridle at this notion, equating it with shameless self-promotion. But the goal here is not to take away from anyone else or do someone else harm. It is not a zero-sum game, but it is the way the game is played.

The goal is simply to get recognized for the great work you're doing. If you don't go out and "market" your work, no one will hear about it. It doesn't matter how good your work is; if you remain in obscurity you'll be hard pressed to get grant funding (and to achieve just about anything else you want to accomplish that involves other people investing in you).

To get started, take out a piece of paper and a pen, and do the following exercise:

First, take inventory of your marketing activities. This may include your website, keeping that site up to date with current articles about relevant topics, your publications in scholarly journals, your books, your speaking engagements, your networking, and so forth. Take five minutes to write down your inventory.

Now review the list, and identify the biggest "gap" in your efforts. For example, if your website is woefully out of date (or non-existent), that might be your gap. Now, spend another five minutes making a brief plan for what you're going to do right away to start filling that gap. All progress is made one step at a time, and by moving forward on this you are taking an important step forward.

"Who" is represented uniquely in your proposal

All sections of a fundable grant proposal must include "Why" → "Who" → "What" → "How". This sequence is discussed in Chapter 11. However, "Who" is special, in the sense that it is both a step in the process to funding, and also an all-encompassing "bubble" around your work.

If you are a Nobel laureate, there will be a "halo" around your proposal as soon as your reviewers find out about your status. You won't be able to get away with a proposal that lacks one of the other elements, but when reviewers encounter your Why, What, and How, they will likely be received with more positivity and enthusiasm.

On the flip side, if you are an "unknown" to the reviewers, your proposal sections will be received with more skepticism. To achieve funding, your proposal must be all the more excellent.

So, if the "Who" bubble encompasses all of your work, why is it also included as the second step?

Because when writing your proposal, you must mention yourself and your accomplishments, albeit briefly. This is especially true if you're an unknown.

Your proposal will first cover the "Why" to hook the reviewer and get her interested. Next you'll convince her that you are credible, and capable of accomplishing the proposed task. Here, you'll mention past projects or accomplishments that are directly related to the project at hand. If you are writing an academic grant proposal, you'll cite a few of your papers here. *Peer reviewed papers are a powerful form of social proof.*

Often, you can intertwine this "Who" part with the "What" (next chapter). You start discussing the "theory" of what it is you're trying to do, and bring in references to your past contributions in that regard. That is a great way to bring in "Who," <u>without appearing boastful.</u>

You must discuss the "Who" early on in your proposal, but you also want to avoid signs of chest-pounding or bragging. This will turn people off; they will see it as self promotion. As mentioned above, use indirect statements about your accomplishments that are intertwined with the "What" part of your proposal. Discuss your accomplishments in a few sentences, and in a matter-of-fact manner.

For example, in a proposal to the National Institutes of Health, the "Who" will be briefly mentioned as a few sentences in the Specific Aims of the proposal. In the Significance section, you'll expand on that, including a paragraph or so on your experience as it relates to the proposed task. Again, write this as a matter-of-fact piece in the third person, as if someone wrote it about you (not like you were writing about yourself). This will minimize the chances of you setting off reviewer's "self-promotion" alarm.

SPECIFIC THINGS YOU CAN DO TO PROVIDE SOCIAL PROOF IN YOUR PROPOSAL:

1. **If the grant agency allows it, get letters of support from other people in your field and include them in your proposal.** Find people who may be interested in the outcome of the work that you're proposing to do, and ask them for a letter. Don't be shy - many of us are far too timid about asking. Sometimes we will get a "no" answer, but if we keep trying, we will get some "yes" answers too. The important point is that the reviewers don't know about the "no" answers you got! They will only see the letters from people who said yes to you. When you ask for a letter, be prepared to write a draft of it to save time for the letter writer.

2. **Highlight your past track record, making sure that you indicate recent grants that have been funded in the same area.** This is another form of "social proof" - if other reviewers have given you grants, this adds "proof" that you have the credibility to do the work that you say you will do. This is why if you're starting from nothing, it is harder to get funding than if you've had funding before. If you're new to grant writing, this is a very good reason to seek out your first grant from a source who focuses on small awards for "newbies." For example, in the sciences, the National Institutes of Health and National Science Foundation both offer various types of early career awards. It is far easier to get one of those the first time than a regular grant - and then you can use that to build upon. Another way to do this is to seek out other small awards in your field. Even if you only get a grant for $5,000, putting that as part of your track record will support the cause that you're doing something worthwhile.

(Continued next page)

3. **Get out to meet people in your field.** Go to conferences and meetings. Volunteer to be a grant reviewer. Invite them to visit you (e.g. if you're at a University, invite others from your field to give talks). When you interact with others, show excellence in what you do.

4. **Become a recognized thought leader.** This can be done many ways, but the most important mode is through writing. If you're in academia, this comes from writing great scholarly articles and/or books that define your field. If you're in another area, write blog posts and other online articles. Lead the way with your ideas using the written word. If you are not adept at writing, then hire someone to help you with this aspect. It is vital that you present yourself well through the written word. With the advent of newer internet technologies, you can add in video, audio, and other forms of communication that show you have something to offer.

CHAPTER 10

What is the theory behind your request?

You've explained to your reviewer and funding agency WHY they should support your work, and WHO you are to be trusted with the money. These two vital steps must come first (and many people overlook them), but they are not all there is to be said.

Behind any proposed project there must be some theory of how the world works, and how your project will intersect with that theory in order to make the world a better place. The What is that theoretical description -- that model.

Let's use an HIV vaccine as an example to illustrate the Why, Who, and What parts.

Why: Because many people continue to die from AIDS, which is caused by HIV, and because there is no functioning vaccine to reduce those deaths.

Who: An established retroviral researcher who has a track record developing vaccines for other related viruses.

What: HIV attacks lymphocytes and T-cells, disabling the body's immune response. It is difficult to develop a vaccine because the virus mutates so rapidly, and because it evades the initial immune responses typically prompted by a vaccine. Hence, any successful vaccine must take a different approach than the standard one, and our approach is...

I didn't finish that last part of the What, because that will be very specific to the research. I'm also not actually an HIV researcher with a potential vaccine to offer. But hopefully this illustrates the point for you, and helps you understand that what goes into your model of the world, and the basis for your project.

Your model of the world needs to fit your reviewers' model

The grant review process favors evolutionary work over revolutionary work. In other words, your proposal must contain a model that is commonly accepted by your community. Most granting agencies will find one or more reviewers with expertise in your area to read your proposal. If your model of the world differs from that of the "prevailing wisdom," you must present it carefully.

Saying, "Here is my model, and it is a better model than everyone else's," will raise your reviewer's defenses. This won't work in your favor. (Yet I see people doing this all the time.)

Often we are are so stubborn, and believe so strongly in our own model of the world, that regardless of the potential penalty, we go write about our model as if we <u>know</u> it is right.

A much better approach is to step back and realize that nobody's model is "correct." Models of the world constantly evolve, including scientific models, social models, psychological models, and so forth. What was accepted as "the truth" 30 years ago is usually much different from today's accepted "truth."

Your model may be different and better (at least in your mind) than the prevalent model. But even if it really is, you must realize that it will take many years and a lot of work on your part to convince your peer group of its viability.

You cannot go around presenting the model in a chest-pounding, "I am right" manner and expect people to: a) believe it, b) give you money to pursue it, or c) restore your professional reputation if you are mistaken.

Instead, use the art of framing to carefully couch your model with respect to the prevalent models that most people hold.

Let's consider this in the context of the HIV example. Say that the prevalent theory for why vaccines don't work is because of the virus' high mutation rate. The virus changes so rapidly over time that, anytime you develop a vaccine, it morphs to a different form that is no longer targeted by that vaccine.

Your belief is that the recent attempts at HIV vaccines haven't worked due to the virus' dampening effect on the immune system. Your notion is that HIV thwarts the immune system before it can mount a defense (and all vaccines rely upon the immune system of the host to mount a defense.)

You have some good evidence for your model being the "real reason" an HIV vaccine hasn't worked.

If you write a proposal to develop a new HIV vaccine based on your theory, you have to frame it carefully. If you simply say that the "mutation theory of HIV vaccine development is wrong" and then proceed to present your alternate theory, your reviewers will become more than a bit unhappy with you. Their defenses (egos) will be raised, and they become hostile toward anything else you have to say. That doesn't translate to funding.

Instead, discuss both theories, presenting them both as neutrally as possible. Then point out that the "problem" of developing a vaccine is still unsolved. This will lead the reviewer to conclude that some flaws in the current theory may have been overlooked. This is much more effective than simply pointing out that a current theory is flawed. **Let the reviewer come to that conclusion on her own!**

Once the reviewer has accepted your point and agrees with you about the flaws in the current theory, you can gently introduce your new theory. But don't say that it is an alternate/better theory

- simply present it as a new model worth considering in light of the available information. It is even better to use the existing model to support yours – as a natural extension, if you will.

Then show as much data/evidence/information as possible to support your model, without coming off as overly invested in it. This is a key point. Yes, your goal is to convince the reviewer of your model's viability, but if you are blatant in your approach, you'll get your reviewer's defenses up. When that happens, your chances of getting funded begin to slide.

You have to walk a fine line between showing enthusiasm for your work, and proving that you are relatively unbiased and independent. You have to demonstrate that you aren't too vested in your model, and that you aren't trying to change the reviewer's mind about his model of the world.

In other words, "Stand on the shoulders of giants!"

The best way to do this is by playing the role of "impartial observer" when you're writing. Instead of writing your proposal from your perspective, consider your your model and the problem it presents from a rational, uninterested perspective. If you can adopt that perspective, even for a short period, it will be much easier to write about your theory in as unbiased a fashion as possible.

The one thing you can do to greatly increase your chance of funding

I started writing funded grant proposals as a graduate student, back when I had no clue what I was doing. I attribute early successes to several things:

1. Great mentors who helped me with my proposals.

2. An easier funding environment (compared to now).

3. My ability to put myself in the mind of the reader.

It's not easy to step out of your own mind to see things from the reader's perspective, but this talent is key to writing a great proposal.

This derives from the lost art of listening. Popular culture places no emphasis on this art. We sit around in classes and lectures a lot, ostensibly "listening," but it's a self-centric sort of listening. In these environments, we are listening with the goal of gaining some knowledge for ourselves - not with the goal of better understanding where the other person is coming from, and in particular, what they want.

Good listening, where you try to deeply understand where others are coming from, is a key starting point for knowing where your reviewers are coming from. The goal is to understand what gets them excited. What theories are currently popular? What problems need solving? If your proposal provides solutions to current problems, you will have far greater chances of funding than just proposing what you want to do, with no regard to whether anyone cares or not.

This doesn't just pertain to grants. Let's imagine two retail businesses in a downtown area. One is called Gloria's Razzletazzle. You walk by the storefront, which has some odd assortment of relatively unrecognizable items in it, like odd birdhouses and such.

You're not really sure what Gloria is trying to sell, but it doesn't seem to fill any need that you have, or solve any problem you're having. So you move on.

Just down the street is Joe's Java Hut. On the roof is a 20-foot, stylistic coffee cup made by some creative metalworker. You are a coffee fanatic, especially since you like to work 20 hours per day on frequent occasion (like when you're writing your grant proposal). You instantly recognize that Joe potentially has something you want, and stop in to sample his stuff (I mean, coffee - what were you thinking?). If he provides you with a good product, you're likely to come back - maybe a few times a day!

Who is going to get your money, and why? Clearly for most people, the answer is going to be Joe. The occasional person who wanders past Gloria's place may go in out of curiosity, but there is a fundamental difference in the approach that these two businesses exhibit. Joe knows who his audience is and what they want, and his business is focused on making it clear to that audience that he has something for them. As a result, Joe gets most of the business.

Gloria doesn't seem so clear on who her audience is or what problem she's solving for them. Her store is based on her own interests in unique and unusual items from small mom and pop craftspersons. She picks up the goods on her trips around the country in her RV. It's not that these items would be impossible to sell. In fact, there's an audience for these items. However, she is doing a poor job of connecting with that audience through her storefront display and store name.

When you're writing a proposal that you want people to fund, you're facing the same challenge as these businesses, but with one twist: In a business, you can define who your audience is, and then go about trying to attract that group to buy your stuff. With a grant, the audience is usually predefined for you.

You may have some leeway in the audience selection by choosing the particular review group or study section that your proposal is sent to. Some agencies, like the U.S. National Institutes of Health, will give you some choice in this matter. Your choice will at best consist of two different review groups that your grant could be sent to, and at worst you have no choice in the matter at all.

Since your proposal will be sent to this predefined group that you have no control over, your only option is to find out what that group wants from you, and then do your best to provide it to them. The appropriate business analogy might be trying to open a business in a strictly-controlled, dictatorial economy, where the government has the predisposition to tell you what kind of business you are going to run and where you are going to put it. You'd have to figure out who is walking past your business everyday, and how you can provide those people with something they'd want (within the bureaucratically-defined guidelines).

The best way to deal with this is to **listen, understand and put yourself in the "customers'" shoes.** You need to understand them better than they understand themselves.

The same goes for your proposal. The deeper you understand what your funding agency, and the reviewers who are hired by that agency, the better your proposal will be.

The problem is that most of us are so embedded in our own experience and knowledge that it is very hard to step outside and see our work the way another person would see it. Yet doing this is an incredibly valuable skill. If you can see your work as another human sees it (one who does not have your expertise) you are far more likely to be able to improve it dramatically so they understand it and become interested in it.

Here's one way you can trick your mind into seeing things from another perspective: Close your eyes and picture yourself outside of yourself, and even better, picture yourself becoming someone else that you know (such as a peer who might be reviewing your grant). Become an actor in your mind, taking on their knowledge and persona. I know this sounds weird, but again, you are simply playing a trick on your mind to help it forget what you know, and see things from another point of view.

Now, once you're firmly in that mental space of "being someone else," look at your proposal's specific aims, summary, or abstract. How does it sound now, when you are that other person? Does it make sense? Is it too pushy? Is it full of buzzwords? Immediately write down your impressions, before you lose your "independent observer" perspective. Hey, if this all sounds too weird and woo woo, you can just skip it, but you will be missing out on a new viewpoint on your proposal that will help you make it better.

If you decide to take this seriously, you'll probably have to repeat the exercise several times to get to the point where you can become truly independent of yourself. It helps a lot if, after you write something, you put it away for a while, and then come back later for an unbiased look.

Why is this in "what?"

I put this advice in the "What" section of the book because it's where you'll most likely get lost in the details of your own knowledge. In terms of the mental ratchet, we proceed like this:

Why: This is the first step of getting your reviewer emotionally onboard with you. You want them excited, enthusiastic, and interested. Without that, not much else matters.

Who: You want your reviewer to overcome that first reaction to their enthusiasm, which is, "Okay, sounds great, but can they really do it?" All decisions that are made by humans start with an emotion, and are later justified by rationality. So the reviewer is looking for rational justification that you can do the work.

What: You're drilling deeper into the rational justification for the positive emotional response you prompted with the Why. You're trying to justify a reasonable and rational model of the world, and of the problem you want to solve with the grant funding.

Usually, conflicts over models of the world occur at that last step. The conflicts can occur even in the "Why" part, but that's less frequent. Nonetheless, you have to pay attention to the possibility of conflict throughout the proposal. To get there, consistently practice the visualization exercise of going outside of your own mind, and get into the reader's mind. Practice listening at conferences, talks, reading papers and so on. Find out what gets people excited, and what does not. The more you can interject your work into that stream of excitement - whatever it is - the better off you'll be[7].

Innovation lies in Your "What"

We discussed innovation in the "Why" section of this book, because most reviewers get excited about innovative new approaches to solving problems (more so than they get excited by the same old way of solving a problem). But at its core, innovation is directly part of the "What," or your model/theory/hypothesis of the world, and of the problem that you want to solve.

What makes a proposal innovative is the process by which you overturn old models, and present new and different models that may have a better chance of solving the important problem at hand.

---

[7]   *You may have some groundbreaking project you're working on that is outside of the mainstream right now. I'm not advocating that you just drop that project. By all means, keep it going because that is where a great deal of progress comes from. However, don't be under the illusion that you will get a lot of funding for this from the more conservative agencies (like the NIH). If your work is presently far outside the mainstream, getting it funded will be a big, uphill slog right now. So get some other more mainstream work funded, and then piggyback your groundbreaking work with it.*

Theories constantly change and evolve. You will be seen as innovative if you are on the leading edge of that evolution, and if you are pushing forward with new approaches, models and theories of how things work. Most importantly, you will be seen as innovative if you push forward with new **solutions** to longstanding problems (solutions which are usually based on a different model).

We previously discussed the LifeStraw's innovative approach to providing clean water to people in impoverished countries. This device was innovative because it used a different model of the world. The previous model centered around providing a centralized source of water to a whole village or community. But that presented many complications, such as how to power the water source, how to maintain the water source, and so forth. The LifeStraw inventors developed a **new model:** generating clean water on an inexpensive, portable, individual basis where and when it is needed. In other words, it was a fundamental shift from a centralized to a distributed model of water generation.

Any model shift has both advantages and disadvantages. However, if the apparent benefits of your new model are greater than its drawbacks, then you'll be considered innovative.

It's difficult to be seen as innovative if you're following everyone else's model. To be innovative, you have to go outside of or beyond the models of the world held by your peers and find a new and more useful model.

Not every type of grant proposal requires innovation at its core. Some encourage innovation more than others do. However, innovation can boost your grant funding chances because it shows that you aren't doing exactly the same thing others have done, and you aren't trying the same things others have tried.

That said, innovation is a fine line. As we discussed earlier in this book, contradict your reviewer's model of the world too much and you will raise her defenses and set her mind against you.

The target group's organizational culture also comes into play. Some cultures are very conservative, others are less so.

When you come up with a great idea for a new model, make a serious effort to test it before you present it to any review panel. Preliminary evidence of your model's validity - proof that your innovation will pay off - goes a long way in convincing a skeptical audience to believe you may in fact pull it off. Promote your new model through papers and presentations so that people are actually starting to buy into your new model. Skip these steps and your attempt to get funded may be challenging.

"What" is <u>not</u> a long and boring summary of everything everyone else has already tried

Particularly in academic circles, many grant writers use the "What" as a literature review. They create documents that trace the development of a field of study from inception through all of the different stages, citing the many developments (and papers) that have occurred along the way.

This makes for an incredibly boring "What," and the first principle of effective grant writing is that **"thou shalt not bore thy reader!"**

Few reviewers have the time and/or interest to learn about everything that has been tried and didn't (or did) work out. They are not reading your grant proposal for a history lesson. They are reading your grant proposal because they're trying to figure out whether it will be a good investment.

Trust me, you don't look any smarter or wiser when you show those reviewers that you've read up on your history. It only makes you boring and pedantic. We've all had teachers who were boring and pedantic, and we can attest that such instructors are rarely a source of enthusiasm or excitement.

INNOVATION AND VARIOUS
FUNDING AGENCY TYPES.

The National Institutes of Health (NIH) has a very conservative reviewer culture. In fact, it is the most conservative of any I have encountered. In this culture, any presented innovation always has to be balanced with a strong dose of feasibility (i.e. showing that the idea is not only good on paper, but good when actually tested in the real world).

The National Science Foundation is a bit less conservative than the NIH. It requires less evidence of feasibility and prize innovation, yet it is still conservative enough that without some evidence of feasibility, there is not much hope for funding.

For these scientifically-focused review panels, you'll typically want to conduct preliminary experiments that provide some data to support your new model of the world. At bare minimum you'll want to provide some strong arguments/data from the scholarly literature about the validity of your model.

In my experience, the least conservative panels are those where businesspeople are involved. People in business seem to prize innovation and "great ideas" more, and don't need as much proof of feasibility as the more conservative scientists. That doesn't mean you can come up with a wild idea, with no evidence that your idea will actually work, and get funding. Even with businesspeople as reviewers, the panel will want evidence that your new model or innovation has some chance of working. In this case, you will want to develop a prototype and test market it. Or you'll want to perform surveys of potential clients/consumers.

No matter who the audience is, to sway reviewers you must present evidence supporting the validity of your new model for the world.

Think about your past teachers for a moment. Who were the best teachers you ever had? Were they the ones who did a long review of the "facts" in the field they were teaching, presenting one after another in endless succession? Or were they the ones that got you involved and engaged, and interested in figuring out and solving some interesting problems/conundrums/puzzles?

In my case, it was definitely the latter. I doubt many people will choose the former.

In your grant proposal, you want to be like the latter educator, and not like the former. It's not that you can't present any history from your chosen subject, but you want to present it carefully, and in an interesting and engaging manner.

In this sense, you have to refer back to the first step: Why. For each "fact" you present as part of the What, you have to make it clear Why you are presenting it. This starts with asking yourself why you want to present it, and getting clear on that. You should not present any facts or historical details for which there isn't a clear, "Why am I including this?"

A significant part of good grant writing is knowing what to exclude, not just knowing what to include. You must be ruthless in your exclusion of facts or details that are not relevant to the central mission of getting the funding you need for your work.

Remember that working on a project for a long time is never a sufficient "Why" for its inclusion in your proposal. The "Why include it?" has to be relevant from *the reviewer's point of view.* They don't care how hard you worked. They only care about whether this will be a good investment!

In your grant proposal, present the predominant model of the world, and then discuss how your model differs from that. Highlight what's new/unique about your theory/model/approach from a big picture perspective. Make sure it's relevant only to the present moment in time, and not based on what was going on 10 or 20 years ago. These dated perspectives won't help your reviewer decide whether your proposal is a good investment or not.

Be sure to avoid a boring, long-winded, and tedious overview of your field, but do introduce at least some information about existing model(s). Acknowledge the work of others in the field, and provide contrast for your own model of how things work, or how the problem will be solved.

How to address the "What" in your proposal, summarized

The following pages provide a simple recipe summarizing everything we've discussed about your What.

1. **Regularly practice putting yourself in the mind of your reader/reviewer.** Visualize going outside of your body and being an independent observer. Alternatively, visualize being someone else that you know. Think of yourself as being your friend or colleague reading your proposal. How would they react? The more you practice this, the better you'll get at grant writing.

2. **Make sure to have others read your work, even after you get really good at #1.** Other people will always notice things that you overlooked, such as flaws in logic, statements that don't fit, bad grammar, and so on.

3. **Present a new or alternative model for how things work or for how you will solve the problem, in order to be considered innovative.** Practice brainstorming and thinking "outside the box" to come up with new and unique solutions to problems, rather than just following conventional wisdom.

4. **Present your new model/theory/innovation in a carefully framed manner, so that it doesn't raise your reviewer's defenses about their own existing model of the world.** Do not present your new model from the perspective of "hey, my model is better than yours," but instead as "here's an alternative model that might be worth considering, with the following potential advantages and disadvantages". Those are two different ways of saying fundamentally the same thing, but those will elicit very different responses from the reviewer.

(Continued next page)

5. Make sure to collect some preliminary evidence or build prototypes of what it is that you want to do, to provide data in support of your new model. While it is very important to innovate, it is also very important to have evidence that your innovation has a chance of working. Your reviewers and funding agency usually don't want to gamble on wildly hopeful ideas that have little chance of success. This is true even for proposal mechanisms that claim they focus on "high risk/high payoff" ideas (like the NIH R21 mechanism). You still need some solid rationale for why/how things might work out, or you're unlikely to convince reviewers to invest in your new idea.

6. Discuss the other existing theories/hypotheses/models of your field to give some perspective, but do not go into a long, boring historical review of all the preceding developments.

CHAPTER 11

Describing "How" you will change the world

We've gone through a three-step process of creating an emotional basis for your reviewer's decision, (i.e. the Why - excitement and enthusiasm) and developing the rational Who and What elements. The final step is to make the proposal concrete by presenting a specific recipe for getting the project or the work completed.

There is a fundamental oddity with this step: You are expected to present a recipe for how things will work <u>before</u> you get a chance to test the recipe. In essence, you must be able to create your end product before one of the foundational elements -- the funding, that is -- is even in place.

Imagine doing this for a bakery. You're asked to come up with the recipe for a delicious new pastry, but all you have to go on is guesswork and past experience. You can't actually test the recipe you come up with until <u>after</u> you've convinced a set of readers that it will be the best pastry they've ever tasted. You've been given money to start testing your recipe for the perfect pastry.

That sounds borderline crazy, but it's how grant funding works. You propose your recipe, and -- if you get funded -- you begin testing it. You'll realize that your recipe has certain flaws that were not apparent to you or your reviewers beforehand. You'll adjust your recipe to get around those flaws. In the real world, this process of testing and adjusting is necessary to arrive at a great end result.

This process is akin to asking the reviewers to use a crystal ball to predict what will work and what won't work. Unfortunately, I don't know anyone who has a crystal ball.

Instead, reviewers rely on heuristics. That's just a fancy word for intuition, emotion, judgement, and so forth.

Going about your proposal process in a rational manner helps those heuristics along.

So, in the pastry example, if you just present your recipe and tell the reviewers "This will be the perfect recipe from the start," will they believe you? Probably not. In fact, you will be looked upon as unrealistic and overly ambitious.

A better approach is to present the recipe while readily acknowledging that it may not be perfect the first time. This will enhance your credibility, and let reviewers know that you are realistic, and not overly ambitious.

These examples beg the question, why not just propose the process for developing the recipe, without ever presenting the recipe itself?

The answer to that question is rooted in basic psychology. While most reasonable people <u>know</u> that no one can predict the future, they also want a good approximation of that future in order to analyze whether it fits with our model of the world, or not. We don't want vague, hand-wavy claims that something great will be developed. We want to see your direction, and how you're going to provide your proposed solution.

Most of us are also oriented towards tangible things. A theory may get us started down the path of rational convincing, but getting us to invest in an idea nearly already requires more concrete proof.

Take a bike shop, for example. If I'm trying to convince you to buy a bike, I will start with the Why: so you get exercise, save on oil usage, and save money. Then I move onto Who: that we are a reliable bike shop with a good reputation. I then discuss the What: that by finding a comfortable bike that is convenient to use, you'll be more likely to ride than if you had an uncomfortable, unreliable model.

Those steps may have piqued your interest, but if you're like most people, you won't be convinced until you actually see a bike and take it for a test ride. You may test ride a demo unit that's "close enough" to the bike you're going to buy, and that may convince you, but until you see a tangible, concrete item (i.e a live bike), you are much less likely to buy it.

The How of your grant proposal is much like the demo bike. It is not the actual bike, but it is a close facsimile. This demo bike must be formulated well enough to be believable and realistic about what the funding agency will get if they give you the money.

How is really about Who

Reviewers want you to use your crystal ball to give them the How because by presenting your chain of logic, they can perform a deeper evaluation of you and your ability to carry out the project. In other words, they want to know if you'll be a wise steward of the money.

You might think that decision could be made based on your reputation, but then Nobel Prize winners would get all of the grants. No one else would ever get any grants. Basing a decision solely on someone's prior reputation isn't enough for most reviewers. They want to know more about your plan.

Your How is a means for the reviewer to look at your logic, your planning, and your thinking in a way that answers the question, "Has this person really thought through this project's difficulties and challenges?"

There will be challenges and difficulties with nearly every project that is worthy of grant funding. As we discussed in the section on "Why," your proposal is usually focused on solving a problem. If it were easy to solve, then the problem wouldn't exist in the first place! Someone would have already solved it. By going after grant funding, you're placing yourself up against a challenge of some kind or another (not just getting the funds!).

The good news is that people are problem-solving machines. In order to write a good "How" for your grant proposal, you have to put on your problem-solving hat and consider the ways you'll solve the problem, plus the potential hurdles you'll encounter along the way.

Your goal is to lay out a logical plan for getting from where we are now, and to a place where the central problem/hurdle in your proposal is solved.

This is vital if you are sending science proposals to an organization like the NIH or NSF, as both have review cultures that have come to expect minute details regarding how you'll make the project happen.

In my experience, non-science grant panels aren't quite as picky in this respect. They'll want a solid plan from you, but it may not be quite as necessary to outline every detail.

This is much like formulating a plan for your next vacation, or a plan for a home or work project. You have to lay out a series of steps, a timeline, and a budget for each of those steps.

This is the straightforward part of most grant proposals. You simply lay out what you're going to do, how you're going to do it, whether you're familiar with the methods being used, and a target completion date.

Don't go into excruciating detail in this section. I've observed many novice grant writers use up the majority of the space in their grant proposal (and the majority of their energy/time for writing) on this aspect. **This is neither the most difficult, nor the most important part of your grant proposal.**

It's not that the How is unimportant. Without a good How, you probably won't get the grant. But by the time your reviewer gets to your How section, they've already made up their minds about whether they're interested and excited, or not. **If you've failed to get them excited by your proposal by this time, the world's most stellar "How" section is not going to change their minds!**

Let's go back to the bike shop. If you've already decided that you don't want to buy a bicycle because you'd rather own a motor scooter, then it is very unlikely that showing you the details of the various bikes in the store will do anything to convince you to buy a bicycle. You've already made up your mind at the "Why" step. It is only once you've proceeded through "Why" (yes, I want a bicycle), "Who" (yes, I trust these people to sell me something), "What" (figuring out what category or type fits my usage) that you will care about details like technical specifications, price points, and payment plans - the "How." **Do not make the mistake of putting too much focus on your How; you will likely fail to get the grant.**

If the reviewers are excited before they encounter your How, then this section simply convinces them that you have a reasonable plan to pull it off. In other words, How serves as a one-way switch: from ON to OFF (but never the opposite).

For our grant funding switch, ON=grant funded and OFF=grant not funded. A solid How section will leave us in the ON state, if it was already in place. If the How section is poor, it will turn the switch from ON to OFF (or leave it in OFF if it was already there). It will almost never flip the switch from OFF to ON!

So tackle your How last. Give it some attention as you're planning your grant, in order to convince yourself that you're not wasting your time and to understand whether your proposal is feasible and realistic. But you don't need to spend a bunch of time writing it out in great detail until you've nailed down the other parts of the proposal.

Here's another reason to save your How until last: It is often defined by the Why. A great grant writer doesn't just come up with an idea and write a fundable proposal in one fell swoop. Great grant writers iterate over ideas. They start with a seed, and refine that seed multiple times during the outlining and drafting process.

It is usually the Why that needs the most refinement because it is the most difficult to pin down. It is the emotional part that answers the question, "Why should the reviewer or funding agency care about my project?" As you refine your project to better align it with that Why, the How will often change as well. You'll be handicapping yourself if you start with a firm idea of the "How" at the beginning, and then allow that to constrain the "Why."

Here's an example from my own work. For many years I have used and developed methods of "proteomics," which are methods for deeply analyzing how proteins function in cells inside our bodies and other organisms.

I submitted several grant proposals to do proteomics on a bacterium that causes frequent infections. But it turns out that proteomics wasn't the best "How" to do that work. There was another approach that was better, and it consisted of sequencing the entire organism's DNA (genome). When we finally gave up our attachment to the proteomics and opened our minds to other ways, the work leapt forward and became more fundable. That's because the Why was to solve the problem of antibiotic resistance. Given that particular Why, proteomics was not the best How.

We haven't abandoned our original How, but now it's just a minor part of the overall project. Why defines our How, but it took several years and rejected grant proposals to get to this point (due to our own stubbornness).

So don't get too attached to your How! Be open to new methods and techniques, and let the Why define them.

Describe the Why of the How

For every method or technique that you will use there must be a clear Why for its use.

In this way, the Why, Who, What, and How formula is a "fractal," and used at multiple scales throughout your proposal. You not only have the large, big-picture Why, but you also have small Whys all over the place that describe the reasoning behind each How. This can be boiled down to a simple rule:

For each How you must have a corresponding Why.

Present a How (method/technique/approach) without justifying it and you risk leaving your reviewer wondering, "Why did they choose that method?" When the reviewer starts wondering, and doesn't get an answer, they will go down a path that you want to avoid -- away from funding your proposal.

Take my work, for example. We were doing proteomics because that's what we were good at, and not because it was the best tool for the job. On multiple occasions, reviewers questioned us with: "Why are they choosing to use proteomics? What benefit does it bring?" We tried to answer that question, and we had some decent reasons for our approach. Fundamentally, however, it was not well-justified as a standalone solution to the problem. We needed other methods. Our grant was rejected because we didn't have a good "Why" for this method.

When describing each approach, be sure to include a Why that clearly describes the benefit of the particular approach you've chosen. If you try to develop a Why for

"Your goal is to take your reviewer on a tour through that future, to get her excited about it, and then convince her that it is believable. To be a good tour guide, you have to get in the habit of layering on the Why and Who. It's just like connecting the dots."

the method and coming up short, then something is missing. You must dig deeper, find another method, or compliment your method with another option. Don't just leave your method sitting there, unjustified. Reviewers will notice this, pick on you for it, and wind up rejecting your proposal.

Leaving things unjustified (without a Why) is a common cause of failure.

Contingency planning

The difference between vacation planning and grant writing is that with the latter, you'll want to pay more attention to contingencies. When planning a vacation, we don't spend too much time thinking about "What will we do if the weather is lousy?"

In your grant proposal, you must plan for bad weather because rain and storms are common in the process. If you are tackling an unsolved problem, there is always bad weather in the form of unexpected challenges, difficulties, or problems.

Your reviewer wants to know that you're realistic about the possible challenges. Neither you nor the reviewer knows exactly what obstacles lie ahead, but it's up to you to identify the most likely sources of challenge, and to describe how you'll deal with them if and when they arise.

In a scientific grant proposal this is often labeled as the "pitfalls and alternatives" section.

I've also used this approach with good results in other types of proposals, including business proposals (where it's known as "contingency planning"). Remember, you are being evaluated by the reviewer for your ability to plan. You must plan not only for the optimal scenario, but also be prepared to manage if things do go as planned.

Let's say you're planning to develop a new electric bike, and you are applying for SBIR (Small Business Innovative Research) funding. The SBIR program is designed to help businesses bring new innovations to the marketplace.

Your reviewers will want to hear about your bike's market potential. Without that potential, there's no reason to develop a product.

To address this topic you may show that consumers buy electric bikes to save money, especially when gas prices are high. You may also show data that correlates the electric bike market directly to increases in gas prices. Your reviewer might be wowed.

That is, until a cranky person chimes in with, "But what if gas prices go down?"

This isn't far-fetched, because they actually did go down dramatically in late-2008 (and I happen to know that bike sales plummeted too).

When the real world intervenes, you get the chance to present alternatives, as follows:

1. Electric bikes are also used by people with environmental and/or health concerns, so we would market towards those people.

2. If we look at oil production curves, it seems unlikely that gas prices will stay down in the long term. In the meantime, we'd slow down spending to "wait it out."

3. The list goes on...

The more potential pitfalls you can foresee, and the more viable alternatives you can present, the more credibility you'll gain. Reviewers will know you've thought through your plan completely, including contingencies.

Drilling deeper into the Who - can you do it?

As we discussed earlier in this book, the How is really about Who. Reviewers are also looking at "whether you can do it" when going over your described methods and techniques.

In the previous section, we discussed that for each How you must have a Why. Here's another rule:

For each How, you must have a corresponding Who.

In other words, there must be someone who can carry out your proposed method/technique/approach. If, for example, you are proposing a new type of cell phone, your team must include a cell phone engineer. If you are proposing proteomic work to study HIV, you must have a proteomics expert and an HIV expert onboard.

This is not a difficult rule to implement, but it trips people up. They include methods they aren't familiar with, for example, and then fail to explain who is going to implement them. A reviewer will notice this and become skeptical about your ability to carry the project through. The switch flips from ON to OFF: no funding.

Even if you're a fast learner who can pick up new methods quickly, it's still important to have an expert onboard who has experience with the particular method/approach (even if you only enlist him as a consultant).

THE LAYERS - AN EXAMPLE

I. Specific aims or project summary - usually one page - it needs all four of Why, Who, What, and How, with the Why leading.

    A. Why - lead in sentences and building up the gap

    B. Who - reference to your past work/accomplishments

    C. What - the model/theory/hypothesis

    D. How - The aims/steps. Each aim includes an implicit or explicit why, what, and who.

        1. Why (as in "why do this aim") should always be made explicit for each aim. Do not just list the thing you'll be doing, make it clear why you want to do it.

        2. The what and who (i.e. what techniques you will use and are you experienced with them?) should also be obvious either in the aim or in the text leading to the aims.

II. The Background/Introduction/Significance section. This section is focused on expanding the Why and What. It sets the frame for the rest of the proposal. Next to the specific aims or project summary, it is the most vital section of your proposal text. Spend a lot of time on this.

    A. Why - Expand on why the agency should be interested in the work: what problem does it solve? What human need does it fill? What Gap does it overcome? Give enough background but not too much. For example, Why might be to figure out how to control hydrogen fusion reactions more effectively so that we can have abundant cheap energy.

(continued next page)

B. What - The theory you're using to address the Gap or problem that you set up in your "Why." For hydrogen fusion, you'd go a bit into the specifics of why it is hard to control fusion reactions, then describe the way in which you think you can solve the problem. This may be a hypothesis you'll test or a technique that you'll use to overcome the Gap. Make sure that you have credibility (the Who) in the area.

C. Who - You say a bit more about why you're qualified

III. The "Innovation" section (if relevant to your agency) - this section is focused on enhancing the Why and the Who.

A. Why - show what's new and useful about your proposal. By proposing a new and hopefully better solution to a problem, you enhance the potential of your work and its interest to the funding agency.

B. Who - In science and technology, being an innovator is seen as an important attribute to have, and showing that you have it will enhance your credibility.

IV. The "Progress Report/Preliminary Results" section - this section, that was previously required on NIH proposals and still used by some foundation proposals, is about the Who and the How.

E. Who - What work have you already done that shows that you have credibility in the field? This is the place to show specific examples. Lots of figures are important here.

(continued next page)

F. How - Your reviewer is assessing whether you have a good shot at accomplishing what you want to do, so the more preliminary evidence that shows you can do it, the better.

V. The "Approach/Research Design/Project Plan" section - this section is mainly about How with some bits of Why, Who, and What. It is usually formed of some introductory text reminding the reader of the "Why and What" (just briefly), then launches into the specific aims of the proposal.

A. Why - Restating what it is that you're trying to accomplish, using new words, to remind the reader of this all-important facet

B. Who - Who should be embedded throughout, as you list the things you're going to do, to show that you are capable of what you're proposing to do (or you have other people who will help you do the parts you aren't good at)

C. What - You will need to mention your theory/ model/ hypothesis when proposing the "How"

D. How - Each aim goes into a "How" you will build or test your model, project, or hypothesis.

   1. Why - Each aim has to show Why it is important to do

For each proposed method, you must either show that you have prior successful experience with that method, or find someone else who does and include them on the project. Be sure to cover this in your proposal.

When describing the proteomics process in the How part of your proposal, for example, you will remind the reviewer once or twice exactly Who will be doing that part of the work (if it isn't obvious). Just including someone in the budget of your proposal, or including their Resume/CV in the biographical section, is not enough! Clearly and explicitly mention them in the How section.

Create a realistic timeline

The reviewer reading your How will determine whether you are realistic, and if your plan is feasible. Many novice grant writers assume they can accomplish much more than what is possible.

For example, if I'm working on a proposal to develop a vaccine for the HIV virus, and I claim that I'll finish the vaccine within the five years of funding, I'll be labeled as overly ambitious. Many other smart, hard-working researchers have worked on similar vaccines for over 20 years, and no effective vaccine yet exists. The community is sure to be skeptical of my 5-year promise.

There is always a disparity between plans on paper and the real world. It reminds me of a house that my parents once built. The architect had put together a fabulous design on paper, but when the contractors went to build the design, the doors clashed when opened in one particular hallway. To fix the problem, the contractors had to modify the design on the fly.

We all have blind spots when it comes to foreseeing problems in the real world. This is particularly true of projects that usually get grant funding, including research projects, product development, and other ventures.

Your reviewer wants to see proof that you understand realistic schedules and timelines. A rule of thumb from the computer programming world is to start with any estimate of how long a project will take to complete, and then double or even triple it. That applies to most research and/or development projects, too.

Some proposal formats ask for a formal timeline, and others don't. Regardless of requirements, you should develop a rough timeline, and be realistic about what you can accomplish.

Include all of the factors that take far more time than you may anticipate, including:

» Hiring personnel for a project. If your project is going to succeed, you must hire good people. Finding the right people takes time.

» Getting supplies for the project. Locating and vetting reliable vendors also takes time. And sometimes, if there are quality issues, you have to change vendors midstream. These problems can add time to your project.

» Purchasing, installing, and testing equipment. Any new piece of equipment comes with a learning curve as you fiddle around with it to get it to operate properly. As an example, my lab acquired a mass spectrometer (a fancy instrument to measure the masses of molecules) for our work, and then we spent over two years getting it to work properly.

» Bureaucracy. If you work in an academic or large institution, the inevitable bureaucracy will impede progress. This can delay hiring, purchasing, and your access to space.

» Space. If your project requires a particular type of workspace, and if you don't already have access to that space, it can take months to acquire it and set it up.

» Employee absence or turnover. If you are relying on employees to do the work, there will issues like extended absences and sick leaves to contend with. If an employee leaves a vital job, it can take months to years to hire and train a new replacement.

» Governmental/administrative approval. If your study relates to drug development, human subjects, or animal subjects, plan for months to years of dealing with bureaucracy to gain the necessary approvals.

Be sure to plan for each of these contingencies, realizing that no matter how smoothly the project itself goes, the external factors will often impinge progress.

These contingencies aren't excuses to delay work; making progress will be vital.

You have to show your reviewers and the funding agency that you can overcome these obstacles while remaining realistic about how you'll jump these hurdles. Remember: you're not going to make the kind of progress that you would in a theoretical "paper" world.

SUMMARY: HOW TO WRITE A GREAT "HOW"

1. Define your big-picture Why first, before going deeply into the How.

2. Let your proposal's Why define the How, not the other way around.

3. Justify each and every approach (How) with a Why. Why are you using that particular approach?

4. Justify each and every approach (How) with a Who. Who on your team has successful, prior experience using that approach?

5. Plan for contingencies. Discuss the most likely avenues of failure, and propose a backup plan for each.

6. Outline your timeline, and try to be realistic. Many proposals suffer from being "overly ambitious" because many of us fail to realize how long getting things done in the real world can take. Scale back your plans if it seems unrealistic for the budget and timeframe.

7. Don't bore your reader with excruciating detail about every little step. Discuss your approach from a big-picture conceptual level, not from the minutiae level. Reviewers don't need to know what brand of hammer you're going to use when any hammer will do.

CHAPTER 12

Putting it all together

Building layers of the four steps to win your next grant

You've learned the importance of the Why, Who, What, and How in your grant proposal, and you know that each element must be presented in a particular order. In Chapter 11 we also discussed that for each How, you need to have a Why and Who. These four elements (Why, Who, What, and How), are layered throughout your proposal, in each paragraph, and in each section. In particular, the "Why" and the "Who" are ever-present factors in all proposal sections.

Therefore, you can't just write one brief "Why" statement at the beginning, and expect to be done with it. Launch into What and How without layering Why or Who on top, and you'll lose your reviewer and get a rejection.

It's kind of like connecting the dots. For example, in your mind you might know perfectly well why you're going to use a mass spectrometer to analyze protein expression in cancer cells. You've been working on that approach for years, so it makes perfect sense to you. For your reviewer, however, the reasoning is anything but obvious.

You have to connect the dots for him. That means you have to explain Why this is the best technology for the job (because mass spectrometers are presently the most accurate way to measure protein expression in cells), and explain Who will be using this sophisticated piece of equipment. You can accomplish the latter by subtly indicating your past experience with the approach.

The skill of layering "Why" on top of all statements is not natural for most of us. We're not used to having to explain "Why" it is that we make a certain decision; we just do it.

But remember, a grant proposal is a prospective piece. It is about the future. Your goal is to take your reviewer on a tour through that future, to get her excited about it, and then convince her that it is believable. To be a great tour guide, you must layer on the Why and Who, connecting the dots for your reviewer.

EXERCISE

After you've written a draft of your proposal, take a break from it for at least two days. Then put on your Sherlock Holmes hat. Visualize being a detective who is sleuthing for Why's and Who's. By doing this mental exercise, you are more likely to step outside your own knowledge, and get into the mode of seeing your work from someone else's viewpoint.

Now read what you wrote. For each statement, claim, or approach that you made in the proposal, ask your Sherlock self: is this justified with a Why and a Who? Is it backed up with a good What? Note down all the places where the dots aren't connected, where you left gaps between where you are and where your reader is. Then, for each gap, connect the dots by filling in the appropriate Why, Who, or What.

CHAPTER 13

Applying the steps to cash in on your next proposal

There are many different types of grant proposals, and the specific details of each type and format are covered in more detail in other resources. Often, the best way to find out is to carefully read the instructions and directions from the agency to which you'll be applying.

Regardless of the funding agency or type of proposal, the four-step formula <u>always applies.</u> That's because it is based in psychology, learning theory, marketing theory, and deep principles that apply to all agencies and proposal types.

I have used this formula successfully on proposals of extremely varied types, including:

- » A business plan for a bike shop that was funded by the town where I lived at the time.

- » A recycling loan fund for a business to make kayaks from recycled plastics from the State of Wisconsin.

- » An exploratory grant from the University of Utah to develop software for analyzing the potency of molecules called "antisense oligos."

- » An NIH award to make a career transition from Computer

Science/Physics over to focusing on the field of genomics, and to start a lab.

» NIH awards for various software development and research efforts aimed at decoding the human genome and proteins in human cells.

» An NSF award to further develop a software resource.

» An NIH award to find new biomarkers for cancer based on a new approach that helps us focus in on the "needle in a haystack."

The list goes on...

I'm not trying to wow you with my accomplishments, but rather to drill in the idea that <u>this formula works</u>.

<u>To help you see the formula in action, here is how it can be applied to grant proposals for the U.S. NIH:</u>

NIH Grants

The U.S. NIH is one of the largest granting agencies in the world, and gives away hundreds of millions of dollars every year for health research. In 2009, the standard NIH grant format was modified extensively from its past incarnation. In the new format, an NIH grant must fit within 12 pages, plus a specific aims page. The main text is subdivided into three sections: Significance, Innovation and Approach. In each section, you'll include each of the four core elements, albeit in different proportions.

New grant writers are usually concerned about repeating themselves by including a component in multiple sections of the proposal. However, when your reviewer reads a whole stack of proposals, the repeated points will be the only ones that stand out.

You can vary the wording to ensure that it is absorbed and remembered. Don't be timid about repeating your core message, which is: Why, Who, What, and How.

Table 1 below includes word counts that will give you an idea of the Why, Who, What, and How proportions in the three primary sections of an NIH grant. You'll notice that the Significance is heavy on the Why component, and light on the How. Because you will include a short preview of your How in this section, reviewers will know what's coming. Also, the Approach section is focused on the How, and will include a brief reminder of Why.

Significance	Innovation	Approach
Why	Why	Why
Who	Who	Who
What	What	What
How	How	How

Table 1: The relative proportions of Why, Who, What and How in each of the sections of your proposal.

The Innovation section is an odd duck in that it includes some of the Why, Who, What, and even a bit of How. Being novel and innovative in your problem-solving will strengthen the "Why," simply because you're trying something new and different (and hopefully better).

Note that the **Specific Aims** for your NIH proposal must balance <u>all four components,</u> beginning with a paragraph or so of Why. Then you'll include a paragraph that goes into both Who and What. The latter two are often combined because you can describe the theory while also detailing your past publications and track record in your theory's development.

Finally. you'll describe the How in the aims, each of which must include a **Why and a How.** Many writers overlook this step, but in doing so they fail to connect the dots for their reviewer, who will be confused over why these specific methods are being proposed. Don't forget to include layers in this section.

You'll wrap up the aims with a brief return to the "Why," discussing the positive impact that your work -- if funded -- will have on the world. To see this in action on a real life NIH proposal, I've made a video and template for you over at *http://grantdynamo. com/getstarted.html*. Once you sign up there, you'll immediately receive an email directing you to the template and videos.

In terms of your grant writing process, make sure that you work on the aims first. Make sure that each of the Four Steps is clearly laid out. **Do not proceed to the rest of the proposal until the aims are solid, and vetted through multiple rounds of feedback from yourself and others.** People who struggle with grant writing usually rush through this step, and write their proposals before the logic of the aims is solid.

Logical consistency is one of the big factors that your reviewer uses to assess "Who" (i.e., are you to be trusted?). It is the little things that count, and one of those little things is this: Whatever you write as actual, numbered aims on your specific aims page should be repeated verbatim in the Approach section. On more than one unfortunate occasion I have reviewed proposals where the aims are spelled out on the first page. When I tried to find those aims in the text, they were obscured. This is self-defeating.

There are many other nuances to NIH grants, but they can be boiled down to a few simple things:

1. The NIH has a problem-solving-focused mentality. You may have a great, revolutionary idea, but unless you can tie it to a real and specific problem that the research community is facing right here and now, your chances of getting funding are slim to none. If you want the funding, you must work on problems that the community cares about.

2. What you work on must tie into human health, human biology, or human well-being. Do not leave that tie-in for your reviewers to guess at. You must make it explicit for them.

3. As with all proposals of any kind, you must start by clearly spelling out the Why (e.g. tie in to human health, a problem being solved, and so forth), show What your theory is and the data you have to back it up (NIH reviewers are mostly conservative), illustrate Who you are, and explain How you'll do the work.

Many people get lost in the details, assuming that an NIH proposal should be very dense, much like a specialist scientific paper. While some technical detail is needed -- particularly in the Approach section -- if you use too much, you will lose your reviewer's interest. You'll drown them in details rather than conveying the "why they should care." You will be done for.

CHAPTER 14

Why your grant was rejected (and what to do about it)

If your grant proposal was rejected, you're in good company. Notices of rejection are more common than notices of acceptance in this competitive arena. If you use the approaches discussed here, you will improve your chances of funding and reduce the odds of being rejected, but you will probably never reduce your rejection rate to zero. Here's why:

1. There are almost always far more grant proposals submitted than there are funds available.

2. Your grant reviews rely upon reviewer judgements, which involve their own particular experience and biases. If one or more reviewers simply don't like what you're offering, rejection is likely, regardless of great your proposal is.

The next time you get a rejection, the key is to **learn from it** and use the experience to reduce the chances of rejection the next time. While many of us enjoy complaining about poor reviews and biased reviewers, such griping doesn't help us solve the core problem: getting our grants funded. In fact, by complaining about it, we are putting the power and control in someone else's hands.

When we complain, we are saying to ourselves: "I have no control over this situation; it is all up to the luck of the draw and my reviewer's whims." We become self-hypnotized into believing that this is true, and wind up in a negative spiral. We think that by writing more grants and "playing the odds" we'll beat the system. Many other people are also taking the same approach, and the whole system becomes overwhelmed by an ever-increasing number of poorly-conceived proposals. Throw enough darts and you may eventually hit the target, but consider how much time you are wasting on this approach.

Why not take rejection as a lesson, and learn everything you can from it? This puts the power and control back in your own hands. Instead of becoming convinced that grant funding is nothing but a lottery (which it isn't), convince yourself that grant funding is an art and skill that you can eventually master.

Does mastery mean you'll never fail? Hardly. Let's use the example of the famous painter, Pablo Picasso, who created many works over his lifetime. Were they all of equal quality and value? By no means. In fact, some were clearly better than others, and are valued more highly by art collectors.

Yet few would argue that he wasn't a "master painter." If you put any work of a novice painter who was "playing the painting lottery" up against one of Picasso's works, the former would likely look shoddy. The only way you can become a painter of Picasso's stature is by practicing, improving, and becoming excellent at what you do.

Grant writing isn't any different. Not all of your works will be a success, but -- like the master painter -- you can continually improve your art to the point where you have more success than failure. It is possible. For example, in the past five years my successes have exceeded my failures in grant writing. Of over 30 grants I've applied for, at least 22 have been funded, well over a 50% success rate. A greater than 50% success rate is high compared to average, but it is not perfect. I don't know of anyone with a perfect track record. To get closer to "perfection" requires an occasional failure. Failure is just a form of feedback needed in order to improve.

Realize that your mindset will be key to your own success at grant writing. Ditch the the "playing the lottery" mentality and realize that your goal should instead be that of continual improvement, which will reduce the odds of your next rejection.

The problem is that when you get a rejection, it's hard to interpret what the reviewers were really concerned about. The next section delves into interpreting your rejection to learn as much as you can from it.

Reading between the lines.

Reviewers almost never tell you what they're really thinking.

Reviewers almost never tell you what they're really thinking.

That is not a typographical error. I wrote it twice so that it would sink in. It took me a very long time to understand this saying from my grant writing mentor, Marshall Edgell. When I did "get it," my grant writing experiences changed. You must understand this concept if you want to truly learn from a rejection.

Reviewers almost never tell you what they're <u>really</u> thinking because, at their core, those reasons are emotional in nature. It comes down to emotions like enthusiasm, dislike, disdain, distrust, trust, boredom, and so forth.

While those emotions lie at the root of all reviewer responses, no reviewer is going to tell you that. It's not considered the proper etiquette to say something like: "This proposal was so frickin' boring that I wanted to put a revolver to my head and to pull the trigger to put myself out of my misery!"

As reviewers, we like to think of ourselves as perfectly rational beings who make logical decisions. Our self image doesn't allow us to admit that emotion is what is *really* at the core of our decisions. Some people do use rational thinking to inform or guide the emotion, and that is a good thing.

But the core problem is that rationality cannot answer the question: Will a project will succeed or not? This would require predicting the future, and nobody can accurately do that. So we have to rely on heuristics, probabilities, and emotions. The best logic in the world cannot overcome this problem.

That's why people, ultimately, must rely on "gut" instincts and emotions when making decisions. Then they will write some very rational sounding words to justify those gut emotions.

Feedback to your proposal is at least one step removed from the core emotion that led to your rejection. To successfully respond to and learn from rejection, you must be able to read between the lines.

Fortunately, almost all negative reactions to your proposal can be tied to one of the four core elements we've discussed in this book. The reasons for rejection will always relate to one or more of your Why, Who, What, and How. Let's briefly examine each of these.

Rejections due to Why

The "Why" part of your proposal is the trickiest because it relies on core values and belief systems regarding what is and isn't important. A rejection based on your "Why" is typically indicated by a poor scoring of your "impact" or "significance" sections, though not always.

If your Why is lacking, reviewers will seem unenthusiastic. They will just pick on you and pick on you some more. The technical aspects may be covered, but the reviewers will sound almost bored with the proposal itself. This can be distilled to one of several issues:

> » You are working in an obscure area or on an obscure solution for which there isn't much present community interest (even if it was previously a hot topic).

» You haven't tied the proposal into solving a human need that they (and the funding agency) cares about effectively, so the reviewers can't really relate to your mission.

» You haven't conveyed enough new or different solutions, so your reviewers don't see your proposal as being innovative.

» You're too focused on "knowledge generation" rather than "solving problems/gap filling." Knowledge generation is not very exciting.

If your rejection is due to a weak "Why," you may have to go back to the drawing board before you resubmit your proposal. You can't just slap a few extra sentences together and expect to fix such problems. You must put thought into questions like, "Who will benefit from this work?" and "What important problem am I solving?"

Asking these questions will force you to take a new direction. As you go through this exercise, remember that funding agencies aren't in the business of funding your work just because they like you; they are in the business of solving specific problems. If you can't work on a problem they care about, then don't bother submitting a proposal to them.

Rejections due to Who

If the reviewers seemed interested in your idea and approach, but are skeptical over whether you could actually carry it out, you have a "Who" rejection. Basically, you lacked the credibility or trust necessary to convince the reviewers that you can get the project done.

Responding to this type of negative review is easier than dealing with a Why rejection. You must build up your credibility and track record in your revision or resubmission. There are several ways you can do this:

» Enlist a collaborator on the project who brings additional expertise to cover your weak points.

» Gain credibility on the topic through outreach efforts, like writing papers, giving talks or presentations, writing books or articles, visiting your colleagues, going to conferences, and so forth.

» Get more preliminary evidence proving you can do the proposed work. For a product development proposal, for example, this could mean building a prototype and doing more extensive real-world testing with that prototype. For a science proposal, you would want to conduct more experiments to show the validity of your proposed direction.

There's another common reason for a "Who" rejection: Competition. In highly-competitive grant agencies, your competitors may review your proposals and react negatively. They will immediately be on the defensive, and no longer unbiased and open-minded.

There are two solutions to this problem. First, if you can, ask the funding agency not include your direct competitors on the review panel or study section. Often, they will heed such requests.

Second, write such a stellar proposal that the other reviewers are so enthusiastic about that it overwhelms your competitors' negativity. I once wrote a proposal that garnered three glowing reviews, and one negative review by someone who appeared to be a competitor. Fortunately, the enthusiasm of the positive reviewers overwhelmed the negativity of the competitor, and we got the funding. If you get the positive people excited enough, the naysayers' voice can be drowned out.

Rejections based on What

If you present a particular model/hypothesis/theory of how the world works, and your reviewer(s) disagree, you may get a "What" rejection.

This is a tricky situation, especially if you are going up against a predominant paradigm in your field with a different approach. Let's say you think the difficulty of developing a lightweight portable battery for electric vehicles is that our models of energy storage are all wrong, and you have a completely different direction that you believe will work far better, such as a wood based combustion system. Regardless of whether your idea is "right" or not, reviewers will reject your notions if they hold a view steeped in the predominant wisdom of the time. I.e. if everyone believes that a better battery is the only way to go, then you'll have a big uphill battle getting grant funding for your entirely different scheme, regardless of its ultimate merits.

There are only a few ways that you can effectively deal with such rejections:

» Give it some time. Continue to gather and present evidence that your theory or model is workable to your community, until it becomes more accepted and mainstream, then try again for funding.

» Change the focus of your proposal from your own unique model of the world or the problem, and instead examine the predominant model held by your reviewers. Propose to examine some "gap" or "problem" in the latter that no one else has solved. Use that gap as an entry point for your alternative theory. To do this, you must carefully frame your own theory so that it isn't seen as competitive with the current paradigm, but as a small step towards solving the problem.

» Don't be aggressive when presenting your alternative theory. Oftentimes if you have a new theory about how the world works and you just say, "Here's why the old theory is wrong, and here's my new theory," you'll raise your reviewers' defenses (because the human brain gets attached to its models of the world). Instead, take a more unbiased approach. Discuss both the existing paradigm and your new paradigm as if you are a disinterested observer who is evaluating each theory's strengths and weaknesses. Then lay out a goal for delving more deeply into these issues.

Here's a more concrete example: When I co-founded my bike shop, my model was, "Oil will get very expensive, and bikes will be a popular alternative." The model was correct for a short time, but then oil prices dropped. Regardless of my own model, the predominant societal paradigm is that oil is cheap and easy, and that cars are the only way to practically transport ourselves. Hence, I can assume reviewers will respond defensively if I base my proposal on a world where oil is expensive and cars won't be in such high favor.

How would you feel if I told you that you'll probably have to use your car a lot less and ride a bike more often (or walk or take the bus)? Does it make you feel a bit defensive? Good. Whether I'm right or wrong about this prognosis doesn't matter. What matters is the reaction of my reviewer. Knowing this, we must be very careful about how we frame our new and different models of the world.

We must frame the argument in terms of things that people can presently relate to and understand. For the bike shop example, it is much easier to frame the argument around getting more people to bike in terms of the "epidemic of obesity." This is a real and pressing problem with verifiable evidence, and it's more visible than "oil scarcity," for which there is some evidence, but which can readily be debated. In other words, one is an accepted problem in search of a solution. The other is a problem that is only accepted by a minority of people who have studied the data - but even those people do not know for sure what will happen. They don't have crystal balls.

Dealing with a What rejection can be difficult and time consuming. You will need to carefully consider whether it is worth trying again, or whether you should give the rest of the world some time to "catch up" with your new model of reality.

Consider going out for funding for a different area of research while you wait for that change to happen.

Rejections based on How

The How rejection surfaces when the reviewer thinks your specific recipe or approach isn't feasible or expedient. They may like the other aspects of the proposal, but they're not confident in your ability to get the work done. This often is couched in a phrase like "overly ambitious," or it finds a reviewer picking on the specific methods you've proposed. It may also come out if reviewers simply don't see the point in your particular approach, and suggest other alternatives.

Often "How" rejections are tied up with "Who" rejections. It is sometimes hard to separate the two, but it's important to figure out whether you're dealing with a pure "How" rejection (in which case you should change the methods), or a mix of Who and How (in which case you should enlist more expertise).

Dealing with a How rejection can be easy or hard. It all depends on your flexibility. You could run into challenges if you're caught up in a particular technique or approach, and if the reviewers are picking on that inflexibility. The example of my proteomics proposal comes to mind. It took me a few years to "get over" my assumption that I had to use one approach to solve the problem.

On the other hand, if your goal is really to "solve the problem," then you shouldn't be so attached to the particular means of getting there. You should always be on the lookout for the best and most reliable tools for the job, and use them in your proposal. Take this approach and you will arrive at funding faster, and with much less hassle.

CHAPTER 15

One final word
to make you a master

When writing grants, you should always be on the lookout for the best tool for the job. Funding agencies are in the business of solving particular problems or needs, and not in keeping you employed. If you want to stay employed through grants, the best approach is to stay flexible and not get too attached to a particular set of tools or techniques.

Keep your skills and toolsets up to date, particularly in areas that the agency cares about. Don't think of yourself as a microscopist, an HIV researcher, or a river ecology expert. Think of yourself as a problem solver who will always use the best tools for the job.

If you learn nothing else from this book, know that simply adopting this mentality will make a huge difference in your grant writing. Combine this mindset with all of the other approaches you've learned in this book and you will become a master in no time at all.

RESOURCES

Grants.gov - Find and apply for US government grants.

http://www.cos.org/ - A list of funding opportunities for scientists.

http://fourstepstofunding.com/extra - Additional free training videos on the Four Steps to Funding approach.